VIEWS FROM THE
RECTOR'S PORCH

To Lisa + Bill Moore -

Because I think you are
thoughtful, intelligent and
caring. That's who this book
is intended for.

Fondly
Bob Dube

Views from the Rector's Porch

Lessons of a Headmaster

WILLIAM A. OATES

Rector Emeritus, St. Paul's School
Concord, New Hampshire

Selected and Introduced by Todd S. Purdum, '78

POSTERITY PRESS

"The Man Who Cured Polio" (pages 184–85) reprinted by permission of The New York Times Company

Posterity Press, Inc.
PO Box 71081
Chevy Chase, Maryland 20813

Printed in the United States of America

Library of Congress Cataloging-in-Publication Data

Oates, William A., 1916–
    Views from the rector's porch : lessons of a headmaster / by William A. Oates, Rector Emeritus, St. Paul's School, Concord, New Hampshire ; selected and introduced by Todd S. Purdum '78.
        p.   cm.
    ISBN 978-1-889274-45-4 (alk. paper)
    1. Oates, William A., 1916–   2. St. Paul's School (Concord, N.H.)—Biography   3. School principals—United States—Biography.   I. Title.
    LD7501.C678O38 2013
    371.0209742'72—dc23
                                                         2013011945

Page i: The pelican, a St. Paul's School icon, reflects traditional Christian lore that in extremis *this maternal bird will pluck flesh from her own breast to feed her young.*

Page iv: Portrait of W. A. Oates by Everett Raymond Kinstler. The painting hangs in the Music Building of the Oates Performing Arts Center.

*To all past, present, and future
St. Paul's School trustees, faculties,
staffs, students, parents, and
benefactors of this "goodly heritage"*

Grant, O Lord,
That in all the joys of life we may never forget to be kind.
Help us to be unselfish in friendship,
Thoughtful of those less happy than ourselves,
And eager to bear the burdens of others;
Through Jesus Christ our Savior.
Amen.

—"Last Night" Prayer

Contents

Foreword

Many associate the halcyon days of New England's private schools with distinguished leaders: Dr. Peabody at Groton, Dr. Thayer at St. Mark's, Mr. Boyden at Deerfield, Dr. Drury at St. Paul's. Yet, following almost two generations behind, came William Oates, St. Paul's rector from 1970 to 1982, one of the great secondary school leaders of my lifetime.

To say that I'm prejudiced might be an understatement, yet one may understand, since his life and mine have intersected since the start of World War II. We first met in September 1942, he a master, I a fourth former. During the next forty years, through all the crazy changes of location and interests that tend to prune friendships, ours somehow continued to grow.

That's personal, yet not entirely so. Bill has been special for others—not for everyone, I suppose. But I must believe there are thousands out there who feel as I do, and whose private appreciation and affection go unpublicized. One simply cannot stand back a few paces and take honest inventory of the record of St. Paul's between September 1942 and June 1982 without seeing his imprint—stronger, possibly, than that of any other living person. He was always there.

Being there, of course, is not the key. As in anything, one's unique life-giving contribution is the only measure that counts. Bill's was strong and uncomplicated.

He had a single-minded philosophy. If you say you'll do something, don't talk about it, do it. Also, he disagreed with the comment of a rather famous contemporary writer who one day quipped, "If something is worth doing, it's worth doing superficially." Ask anybody: "superficial" wasn't a word you'd glue to Bill. You didn't have to. His was a life of directness, of simplicity.

Bill loved gadgets—even color TV. He enjoyed puttering in the garden, particularly with clippers and a hoe. He liked to swim at the "Y." He loved music—Broadway, classical (mostly Baroque)—and he seldom began work later than 4 A.M.

He wrote voluminous letters to alumni and parents, but never a book. He was a man of distinction but received few honorary degrees. He never gave impassioned speeches. He was never listed in *Who's Who.* He simply was the best headmaster in the business.

During a series of meetings prior to the publication of those brilliant articles in *Daedalus* on secondary education, which Bill organized in 1981, I overheard one of the contributing scholars say, "You know, there is one overpowering feeling I have about St. Paul's School as I look at it juxtaposed to other high schools and independent schools in this country. It works." Not a bad tribute in any age, particularly today.

Why did it work? Many reasons, I suppose, not the least of which was an underlying sense of purpose. The rector was the boss. People looked to him for direction. He gave it and in the process developed a bedrock of philosophy of leadership and management. That's all. He knew where the school was heading.

One of his vice rectors once said, "On Monday morning when I start the week, I run through what needs to be done, what was done last week. I rarely think of anything during the past seven days I would have orchestrated differently. So much time in life is soaked up in redoing things. That's not a problem here. Things 'get done right' the first time. That doesn't just happen; Bill is there—planning, and organizing, and anticipating."

Once (I forget the date) I was eating breakfast at the rectory. I asked Bill what he sensed was the most important characteristic of a successful parent; he'd seen so many. His answer, as usual, went right to the heart of the question: "I suppose, if you could name only one asset, it would be time. When your children need you, they need you now. The best parents I've known are the ones who are willing to drop whatever they're doing simply to be available."

This wasn't an idle comment. Bill never made idle comments. It's what he believed. It's the way he ran the school. Everybody was important.

Most times it is easier to run something new rather than to pull years of tradition onto your shoulders. Bill didn't mind. His own special radar told him the value of what he had inherited in terms of its culture, its intellectual reach, its spirit. His job was to make sure St. Paul's kept moving ahead. How else had it been so successful for more than half of this country's existence? Traditions founder unless they're kept vibrant—rediscovered—rebelieved. He knew this.

Bill is gone now from St. Paul's. But his values remain, and his sense of priorities. They'll still be there for those of us who believe, as he did, in the greatness and the mission of this extraordinary school.

—*Amory Houghton Jr., '45*

PREFACE

William Armstrong Oates's long and influential association with St. Paul's School now exceeds seventy years, a span approaching half the life of the institution itself. His twelve years as the eighth rector, from the spring of 1970 to the early summer of 1982, marked a period of transformation and enormous growth in the life of the school. Indeed, the modern St. Paul's, as the world now knows it, took shape under his steady hand, and his legacy is seen and felt broadly in the school's humane and holistic approach to secondary education; in its embrace of the arts as an integral part of the curriculum; and in its everyday reality as a thriving coeducational institution, ever mindful of its "goodly heritage" but also adaptive and resilient in the face of new challenges, approaches, and ideas.

That Bill Oates should have come to St. Paul's at all—much less have become one of its signal leaders—is in itself a remarkable story. He was born in 1916, a son of the Middle Border in Aberdeen, South Dakota, a town of sixteen thousand people 300 miles west of Minneapolis. His father was a teacher and state college administrator; his mother, one of his father's former students. Oates would later recall watching the sculptures of Mount Rushmore emerge from raw granite, and the excitement of seeing the road that ran past his family's home paved for the first time. Though he trooped widely around the West as an Eagle Scout—from the Badlands and the Black Hills to Yellowstone Park and the Little Big Horn—he had never been east of Chicago when he determined (as president of his high school class of 208 students) that he would attend Harvard College. Against all odds, he did so, spending his summers working in Cambridge and practicing the skills in shorthand and typing (he was "speedy and accurate" on the keyboard by age thirteen) that would later serve him well in composing the writings that constitute this book.

He concentrated in history and Latin as an undergraduate; spent a year after graduation on a scholarship in Europe on the eve of World War II; and then returned to Harvard to earn an M.A. in English history just as Pearl Harbor loomed. A single year as a teacher at Shady Side Academy in Pittsburgh was a brief prologue for what turned out to be his life's work. As an undergraduate Oates had spent some summers as a counselor at Mowglis, an educational summer camp for boys in Hebron, New Hampshire, inspired by the works of Rudyard Kipling and run by Col. Alcott Farrar Elwell, who, as fate would have it, had roomed at Harvard at the turn of the twentieth century with two fellow Cambridge "townies," both of them future rectors of St. Paul's School: Henry C. Kittredge and Norman B. Nash.

Mowglis, also known as "The School of the Open," was more than a conventional camp. Colonel Elwell, a relative of Louisa May Alcott's family of Massachusetts Transcendentalists, was one of the first products of the Harvard Graduate School of Education. His philosophy was broadly progressive, including an emphasis on what would now be called "anti-bullying." A special mission of Mowglis was to help four or five boys (carefully sought out from a camp population of eighty or more) build self-esteem each summer by helping them master some skill for which they had a natural affinity.

In 1942 what Oates would later call "the dazzling influence of coincidence in human lives" led Elwell to put in a good word for him with Nash and Kittredge, and he was hired to teach history at St. Paul's School. Seventy years later, Oates would still be saying "a silent prayer of gratitude for that Harvard undergraduate room" in which his sponsors had lived together. In the fall of 1942, he and his wife, the former Margaret Nichols of Fort Wayne, Indiana, and their infant son, Billy, arrived to take up residence in an apartment in the Upper School.

Soon enough, Oates moved beyond the classroom and into administrative posts that familiarized him with the systems and structures of the entire school, and with its broader community of alumni, parents, donors, and friends. He served variously as registrar, scientifically classifying and codifying academic records; as director of admissions, making a wide circle of acquaintances among applicants and their families, many of them powerful alumni; and finally, under Matthew Warren, as vice rector in charge of the school's budget and business affairs. Widowed in 1965, when Margie Oates died of cancer, and with a family of three boys still in school or college, Oates took a sabbatical to complete his doctorate in education at Harvard, commuting between Millville and Cambridge and adopting the habit—which he would continue throughout his rectorship—of rising in the dark hours before the dawn to work on his dissertation.

As the tumult of the 1960s brought rising calls for change to the school's doorstep, Oates was experiencing the same incipient social revolution firsthand (but at some remove from the school's travails), in Harvard Square. He became a board member of the Sanctuary, an organization engaged in helping runaway youths and community groups and public school teachers develop communication and leadership skills to grapple with neighborhood tensions. Having one foot in Millville and the other in Cambridge during these years, Oates would later recall, gave him a special perspective on the "conflict and seething undercurrents at the School, which were to be relieved only through numerous culture changes."

Oates's doctoral dissertation was titled "The Dynamics of Planned Change," and within twenty-four hours of its completion, the storm that became the "Sixth Form Letter of 1968" broke out at St. Paul's. That three-page manifesto, posted on school bulletin boards like so many copies of Martin Luther's reformist theses of yore, portrayed the school as an institution of mindless rigidity and oppression, lacking "spontaneity, openness, honesty and joy."

When such bursting tensions, and Matthew Warren's own ill health, combined to make the search for a new rector inevitable, Oates's skills and background left him the logical, natural choice for the Board of Trustees, and he was elected in January 1970. (It did not hurt that one of his earliest student friends from teaching days, Amory Houghton of the Form of 1945, was now president of the board.) Together, Oates and the board moved swiftly and strategically to announce that coeducation would commence no later than the fall of 1971. Unilaterally, without consultation, he relaxed such long-standing requirements as compulsory chapel attendance on Sundays and the prevailing dress code of coat and tie for all occasions. In consultation with the faculty, he abandoned the requirement for study of Latin and instituted a new, one-year mandatory study of the arts.

Not without bumps, but peaceably and almost overnight, a new school emerged, one in many ways quite radically different from the old, but one unveiled so carefully, and with such broad support from alumni and the trustees, as to cause barely a whisper of protest among the old guard, who treasured "the enduring values so wonderfully established and honored," as Oates would put it years later.

Paradoxically, it now fell to Oates, whose St. Paul's career had been based on his facility with facts and figures, to become the school's moral and spiritual leader—and to do so, moreover, as but the second lay rector in its history to that point. A coolly thoughtful man whose natural affinity was for numbers now showed himself to be a thoughtfully cool man of words—and of ideas. It is those words and ideas that form the core of this volume. In his person—with his crisp, three-piece Brooks Brothers glen plaid suits, perfectly polished Peal & Co. cap-toed shoes, businesslike tan calfskin briefcase, and spotless ship of a desk in his study on the schoolhouse's second floor—Oates could have passed for one of the CEOs among the board that had hired him. (It bears mention that he gained broad Corporate experience himself, serving on the boards of organizations as diverse as Chubb Life Insurance, the Bank of New Hampshire, and New Hampshire Public Radio.) He continued the school's productive association and exchange program with the Seikei Gakuen school of Tokyo—bravely begun right after World War II—for which he would ultimately be honored by the emperor of Japan.

As he stepped easily into his new role as rector, this professional facade could not conceal a deep and growing sensitivity to the variations of the human experience, and of the joys and problems of young people in particular. Seeking to lead the school belatedly into the late twentieth Century, Oates drew not only on his own scholarly background in educational theory and practice but also on the divergent disciplines of psychology, sociology, psychiatry, and social anthropology, arranging for faculty and student seminars, role playing, retreats, and other exercises aimed at embracing—and educating—the whole person, the whole student, and the whole school. "A considerable quiet revolution had taken place," he would write decades later.

Halfway through his tenure—to the surprise of the school community, his family, and, apparently, somewhat even himself—he conducted a discreet courtship with, and then made a happy and lasting second marriage to,

Jean Matson, the longtime secretary to the director of admissions. Together they presided over Saturday night open houses at the rectory, at which visiting students devoured hundreds of chocolate chip cookies, crackers, and some ten pounds of cheese each week.

Bill Oates's scholarly cast of mind—and his sense of the leadership role that St. Paul's should play in secondary education—were apparent in the way he chose to celebrate the school's 125th anniversary in 1981, near the end of his own tenure. In 1956, on the school's centennial, Matt Warren had commissioned theologian Paul Tillich to deliver an address. Twenty-five years later, Oates chose to sponsor two issues of *Daedalus*, the journal of the American Academy of Arts and Sciences, in recognition "that a well-endowed private school like St. Paul's had an obligation to look beyond itself."

I owe my St. Paul's education very directly to Bill, because his son Billy just happened to marry Muffy Macy, a wonderful woman from my own midwestern hometown, Macomb, Illinois, and they responded to my parents' queries about whether I might benefit from a topnotch boarding school education by recommending SPS. I know I sensed even in my own student days—in the middle of Bill's rectorship—what a remarkable school St. Paul's was, and what a remarkable man must be required to lead it. But I did not understand until I began reviewing the writings that constitute this book the full range and depth of Bill's experience, the subtlety of his thinking about the joys and challenges of adolescence, or the patience and skill with which he nudged St. Paul's into the modern world. Reading these pieces has been like meeting him all over again—and a pleasure.

Some of the essays that follow were composed during Oates's long summer vacation sojourns in England, sometimes in the majestic main reading room of the British Museum. Others were banged out on his typewriter in the second-floor study he had created in the rectory out of what was once an old screened-in porch, the retreat that was always called "the Porch" and whence many of these reflections came. Still others—including an occasional erudite letter to the editor of the *New York Times*—were written in his retirement years in Kennebunk, Maine, and later in Westwood, Massachusetts, where he moved after Jean died. Some of the selections gathered here were written for publication in official school documents and annual rector's reports. Others were composed to be delivered aloud in chapel talks or other community settings. Still others were more private and appear here for the first time in print. Some are quite serious; others are slighter. Some are ponderous; others are sly.

Together, these writings form a portrait—an impressionistic and incomplete one, to be sure—of an extraordinary schoolmaster, who not only led one of the nation's most prestigious and enduring educational institutions smoothly through a time of turbulent challenge and change, but who also did so with a measure of humane and human understanding that should be a model for his school, and for its sons and daughters, for generations to come.

—*Todd S. Purdum, '78*

Acknowledgments

Many dedicated participants associated with St. Paul's School brought this book into being. James M. Frates, '85, conceived and proposed the notion that Bill Oates's thoughts and educational philosophies deserved to be preserved, perpetuated and published. Robert E. Duke, former vice rector and director of development, turned the notion into reality. Douglas Schloss, '77, the president of the Board of Trustees, and Michael G. Hirschfeld, '85, the present rector, expressed their willingness to have the school publicly identified with this effort. Charles Scribner III, '69, recommended Posterity Press, Inc. Philip Kopper, its publisher and chief editorial officer, proved a wise, patient and punctilious guide, working with copy editor Duke Johns and book designer Robert L. Wiser to create this attractive volume. David Parshall, '65, gave an enthusiastic shove to get us moving. A school team consisting of Robert H. Rettew Jr., '69, executive director of the Alumni Association and William Kissick, director of development, provided liaison with vice rector Michelle Chicoine. The school archivist,

David Levesque, offered invaluable help in searching out photographs and documents. Finally, the project depended at every turn on Emily Bruell, who worked as personal assistant to Bill Oates for many months. She dug tirelessly through a vast treasure trove of old papers and files, editing them carefully in conjunction with Bill, laboriously and lovingly typing and re-typing manuscripts, then reading and re-reading proofs with memorable discipline and an eagle eye. Here is proof positive of the ancient truth that success has a thousand fathers—and, in this instance, one mother.

—T. S. P.

Part One

EARLY · YEARS

South Dakota, Harvard, and Professor Matthiessen

This remembrance, sketching Bill's earliest years and college days at Harvard, was composed in the spring of 2012, in his ninety-fifth year, for delivery at Eliot House. In it he discusses an important early mentor, F. O. Matthiessen, the first senior tutor of Eliot House. Professor Matthiessen, a literary critic and scholar of American studies, chaired the university's pioneering interdisciplinary program combining history and literature, in which Bill chose to concentrate. A 1923 graduate of Yale, Matthiessen wrote and edited landmark works on Ralph Waldo Emerson, T. S. Eliot, the James literary family, Sinclair Lewis, Walt Whitman, and others. Remarkably for the time, Matthiessen lived openly in a twenty-year romantic relationship with an older man, the painter Russell Cheney, who died in 1945. Increasingly distraught over the death, and as "a Christian and a Socialist" despairing over conditions in the postwar world, Matthiessen committed suicide by jumping from a Boston hotel window in 1950. His suite at Eliot House remains preserved as the F. O. Matthiessen Room, housing some 1,700 volumes of his personal library, together with manuscripts—including, presumably, the letters Bill mentions. In this talk Bill ascribes to his mentor some of the attributes that made Bill himself a sterling educator.

2

I WAS BORN 300 MILES WEST of Minneapolis, on the high plains of South Dakota, in Aberdeen, a small town of sixteen thousand. The total population of the country then was 105 million. Aberdeen was cold in winter, hot in summer, and a wonderful place to grow up in. The prairie and the westward movement were still fresh.

The grandfather of my next-door neighbor, who was my classmate and closest friend, had founded the town in 1883, having walked twenty miles into the western sun beyond the last road. He placed his walking stick in the ground and proclaimed, "This will be the center of Aberdeen." He proceeded to develop roads, homes, telephone lines, all over the area. I knew him well. He was a determined man.

We had thirty-two members in the Boy Scout troop, seventeen of them Eagle Scouts. I was an Eagle Scout. In the summers we camped all over South Dakota, in the Badlands and the Black Hills. We saw the Mount Rushmore National Memorial emerging from the high granite peaks, as Michelangelo's David had earlier emerged half-finished from that Italian stone. We camped westward to Yellowstone Park, past Wyoming's Devils Tower, returning across the rolling hills of southern Montana, where we inspected the locus of George Armstrong Custer's last stand and other memorable historical locations.

One summer we camped among many of Minnesota's Ten Thousand Lakes, where I jumped across the Mississippi near its source. A hollow, exaggerated claim, you say? Yes, perhaps. But don't forget: you are looking at someone who once, unaided, jumped across the mighty Mississippi River. It is about six inches wide at this location.

I had decided early on that I wanted to attend Harvard College. When the year of my departure for Cambridge approached, our family suffered a sudden, unexpected, and overwhelming sadness: my mother died at the age of forty-five. In the ensuing family discussions, it was agreed that I should tarry longer before leaving home. There were two consequences from this development for me. First, when I did arrive in Cambridge, I moved directly into Eliot House. Second, it was required by Harvard that I decide on my academic concentration before leaving South Dakota.

The Harvard office sent me course description materials and information about concentrations, which I studied. I looked at English literature, several versions of history, at mathematics, which I loved, and other fields. Along the way I spotted an interesting concentration: history and literature. I had five years of study of Latin at this point, and some readings in Roman history. So I became a convert to history and literature.

Reading the materials about the requirements for this concentration, however, left a few questions unanswered. I noted at the end of the printed description of history and literature a small sentence: "For further information, write Prof. F. O. Matthiessen."

I wrote Professor Matthiessen. A reply to my letter came by return mail, which I noted with appreciation. It was a warm, welcoming letter: "I am pleased you are coming to Harvard College, and that you want to concentrate on History and Literature. It is a fine concentration, and you will enjoy it." The letter had carefully expressed answers to my questions, it had come to me promptly, and it was a pleasant, accepting letter. I was very happy.

Nevertheless, study of Professor Matthiessen's letter, along with the printed materials that I had, evoked additional questions. So I wrote him again. Once more, a letter arrived by return mail. In all, I had, I think, five exchanges of letters with Professor Matthiessen, the last postmarked Kittery, Maine.

The day came. I was in Cambridge. I must confess, now, that I did not have a clue about the experiences that were just ahead. I had never been east of Chicago. I had some information about the college's house system, but not its significance. I did not know that, after ignoring the housing needs of students for almost three hundred years, Harvard had just completed building seven small residential units with dining rooms and other facilities at a cost of $12 million. (These residential houses, modeled on the colleges of Oxford and Cambridge, had been underwritten by a Yale graduate, Edward Stephen Harkness, a Standard Oil heir who was also a graduate and benefactor of St. Paul's. Here his gifts not only built the "new" Schoolhouse in the 1930s but also financed the system of teaching around tables that would become known as "the Harkness method.")

I realized I had a friendly helper, F. O. Matthiessen, who had tirelessly answered questions important to me. But I did not know that he had graduated from Yale only ten years earlier, that he had spent several years at Oxford as a Rhodes Scholar, and that he had received his Ph.D. from Harvard in only two years after returning to this country. Matty was one of the brightest lights in the Cambridge firmament.

Rumor had it that four of the seven new houses had actively sought Matty as their first senior tutor. Eliot won out. Thank heavens. Perhaps because Roger Merriman, the first master of Eliot, was one of the five zealots who had created the new concentration of history and literature, the field that had captured Matty's interest.

I moved into Eliot House and, mirabile dictu, I discovered that only several entries away lived Professor Matthiessen. This was fortunate for me. History and literature was a superb concentration—limited to no more than fifty total students in college at one time. (There are now about three hundred concentrators.) But it had limited financial support from the dean of the Faculty of Arts and Sciences. For me, Professor Matthiessen continued to be the principal source of information about requirements and deadlines beyond regular course work. For example, there was a three-hour written examination on eight specified books of the Bible. And a three-hour written examination on eight specified plays of Shakespeare.

There was always a smile on his face, a happy, relaxed demeanor, a welcoming and friendly presence. Not once did Professor Matthiessen pull out a Blackberry or a written daily schedule for consultation and say, "I think I can work you in for five minutes tomorrow at 3:15 in the afternoon." I learned from Professor Matthiessen the effectiveness of instant acceptance and instant response. I learned also that other human values are strengthened at the same time: values of recognition, acknowledgment, support, and friendship. A wonderful human being, Professor Matthiessen.

The day arrived in 1938 when I received my final letter from him. "May 16, 1938: I have the honor to inform you that the Committee has voted to recommend to the Faculty that you be awarded your degree Cum Laude." Signed, beautifully: "F. O. Matthiessen, Secretary of the Committee." It was typed on official stationery of the Committee of Degrees in History and Literature.

I have brought this letter with me tonight, having found it in my Eliot House file. If they will accept it, I would like to give it now to Gail O'Keefe and Doug Melton for inclusion with, I am sure, other Matthiessen memorabilia in the C Entry Memorial Room.

When the Matthiessen Room was established, about twenty years ago, a beautiful stone memorial cutting was made. It is about the size of a large dinner plate and is affixed to the Eliot House exterior wall near C Entry. Through the middle of the memorial plaque, top to bottom, are cut these three words: Teacher Scholar Critic. Each word richly deserved, correctly characteristic of Professor Matthiessen. One word is not there that I would add: Friend. Matty was a wonderful friend to this rookie South Dakota Eliot House student.

—Spring 2012

Mowglis: From Aberdeen to Concord via "The School of the Open"

Bill was deeply influenced by his summers at Mowglis, a pioneering summer camp for boys in Hebron, New Hampshire, which took its name from the Rudyard Kipling character. It was led by Col. Alcott Farrar Elwell, who had roomed at Harvard at the turn of the twentieth Century with two fellow Cambridge residents who would play crucial roles in Bill's life and career. Mowglis, also known as "the School of the Open," was most unconventional for its time. Elwell was related to Louisa May Alcott's family of Massachusetts Transcendentalists, and his philosophy was progressive. A special aim of the Mowglis experience was to develop self-esteem in boys who had been bullied or otherwise disadvantaged, helping them find pursuits at which they could excel.

THREE CAMBRIDGE "TOWNIES" lived together, as undergraduates of Harvard College, in the years 1906 to 1908. One was Norman B. Nash, who became the fifth rector of St. Paul's School in 1940. Another was Henry C. Kittredge, who became the sixth rector of St. Paul's in 1947. The third individual was Alcott Farrar Elwell, director in the 1930s of Mowglis, the School of the Open. It is a strange comment on a strange subject—

8

chance—to say that each of these undergraduates later played a significant role in my life.

Norman Nash appointed me to the faculty of St. Paul's School in 1942, and in 1946 he appointed me registrar of the faculty, asking me to reduce my teaching from four classes to one class to take on administrative responsibilities, and marking a sharp change in direction for my continuance in academic life.

Henry C. Kittredge, a vice rector of St. Paul's from 1928 to 1947, asked me in 1948 to fill in as director of admissions on the illness of Archer Harman, and again in 1950 when Tom Nazro died suddenly. Serving as acting director for six months, and thereafter as director of admissions, gave me a vast opportunity to develop the responsibilities of this office (with the help of others) and a chance to make needed and significant developments in this office.

Alcott Farrar Elwell appointed me to the staff of Mowglis, the School of the Open, in the spring of 1937, when as an undergraduate at Harvard I sought summer employment to earn money for my college expenses. After several summer experiences of considerable success in my eyes, I found myself one day seeking a better academic post than I then enjoyed (in Pittsburgh). When I asked Colonel Elwell whether he could recommend a possibility for me, he said, "I know the current rector of St. Paul's School well. I could speak with him. Do you know St. Paul's School?" I said I did not have a clue about it but had heard of it several times around Harvard. Colonel Elwell made the recommendation, I had an interview, and I was hired by Henry C. Kittredge, acting rector of the school in Mr. Nash's absence (on medical leave after he had fallen while walking on the shore at his summer home in Perry, Maine).

Should I now say a silent prayer of gratitude for that Harvard undergraduate room? For the dazzling influence of coincidence in human lives? Yes. The young, overconfident youth needed opportunities. Fama, Virgil's name for Dame Fortune, smiled on me. I did work hard, but without opportunity (chance), it all would have been different.

It remains to speak of Alcott Farrar Elwell. He had been a lieutenant colonel in World War I and used the title "Colonel" for reference by everyone, making things easy on all sides. He was related to the Alcott family of Concord, Massachusetts. We visited the Louisa May Alcott House, still lived in by family, in Concord several times on our travels to Mowglis and back. His was a family of artists; his father, as I remember, was a painter. Growing up, he lived some years in Europe and some in Cambridge, where, I am sure, Nash, Crocker, and Elwell became friends.

Colonel Elwell began working at Mowglis in the 1930s, under Elizabeth Ford Holt, the remarkable woman who had founded the camp. By 1937 he was camp director and, to all appearances, owner.

With winters free for graduate study, Colonel Elwell was one of the first students in the Harvard Graduate School of Education, receiving his doctorate in 1925. I remember clearly that his thesis had the title "The

Summer Camp as an Educational Institution." His writing on this topic came early in the literature of American education.

The special mission of Mowglis was to help four or five boys, each summer, not only to have an enjoyable summer but also to learn skills and means to assist in their personal development. These campers were deliberately chosen, after careful winter searches, from youngsters aged twelve to fourteen who were, in the current vernacular, being bullied. They were boys who had not learned how to fend off unwelcome aggression from others, who needed to build confidence, pride, and self-respect.

The colonel's method was simple: once camp had begun, to develop an understanding of the campers' problems by the counselors (who, if new, were surprised by this part of their responsibility); then to conduct a relentless search for some camp activity in which each of these campers had a natural affinity; and finally, with tremendous effort, attempt to make each one the "best camper" in this pursuit. Badly needed praise and positive recognition would follow, and a possible glimmer of learning would have been found.

The camp had more activities than I would have thought existed, from bead work to rifle shooting, all forms of woodworking, and so on. A remarkable series of individual searches would thereby be interposed on the normal camp lives of the other eighty campers: mountain camping, canoe trips on the Saco River, on and on. Each activity was the responsibility of a well-trained, well-educated counselor (usually Ivy League).

It is now evident to all that Colonel Elwell was a remarkable man, a fine educator, a man who devoted his life to a series of young boys in a determined quest to help each develop qualities of personality and being to live better and with greater satisfaction in our world, which so often lets each of us down. "The water is the greatest pleasure and represents the greatest danger" was a typical Elwell statement, made to counselors and still clearly resounding in my mind. Each summer was a constant learning experience—along with pleasures such as having a good doubles partner in tennis and many furious games with our rivals, climbing Mount Washington, on and on.

I could easily have gone, long ago, to a summer camp that was solely a camp—a good institution, no doubt. Mowglis was something extra. Chance took me there. Hurrah for Dame Fama.

—July 9, 2012

The Bombing Survey, Spring 1945

Bill arrived in Millville with his wife and firstborn son in the summer of 1942, months after Pearl Harbor, and was quickly caught up in the obligations of school and family life. But at some point, as he recounts in this recollection, written in 2012, it occurred to him to wonder what he could do for the war effort beyond teaching mathematics at St. Paul's School. So he raised his hand and, through an altogether improbable chain of circumstances, eventually found himself—thanks to his fluency in German—attached to the U.S. Strategic Bombing Survey. This independent board of experts had been established by Secretary of War Henry Stimson, pursuant to an order of President Franklin D. Roosevelt, to gauge the effects of Anglo-American bombing on Nazi Germany. The survey was chaired by Franklin D'Olier, the head of the Prudential Insurance Company, who had been the first national commander of the American Legion after World War I, and its directors included such future architects of Cold War foreign and economic policy as Paul H. Nitze, George W. Ball, and John Kenneth Galbraith. The survey would find that the air war in Europe, up to V-E Day, had cost the United States more than $43 billion and 79,265 lives (and had taken a comparable toll on the Royal Air Force). The devastation of the "battered towns of England and the ruined cities of Germany" would

remain vivid for Bill more than sixty-five years later. This cataclysmic ruin was summed up for him by the haunting image of a lone five-story house standing in the wreckage of London's East End, bearing a sign "with the most graphic short message I have ever seen: 'Welcome Home, William'"—a surviving building welcoming a surviving soldier.

I N LATE AUGUST, 1942, Margie and I, with Billy, had arrived at St. Paul's School, to join the faculty and take up residence. My draft board in Cambridge, Massachusetts, had not called me to other national service, and I had not been drawn, voluntarily, at any earlier time to military or other forms of service. Military life had never interested me.

At this stage of my life, with Harvard A.B. and A.M. degrees behind me, as well as a year of study at Freiburg im Breisgau, Germany, and in Paris, I was confident that I could teach almost any subject save the sciences, and I imagine I thought I could do this not only with satisfaction to students and institutions but with distinction. I remember my early resumes listing history, mathematics, Latin, and other languages, ending with the word "Other" laying out a breathtaking array of further possibilities I regarded as easily within my grasp. If enthusiasm, ingenuity, and a minimum learned competence in such an array of subjects could be combined with willing hard work, there was an element of truth in this confidence. The passing years would see adjustments to this point of view, but of course, as things turned out, I spent only four years in full-time teaching before administrative tasks arrived.

I had arrived at St. Paul's engaged to teach history, but soon, perhaps the second year, a vacancy in the Mathematics Department appeared. Someone had noted mathematics in my string of available subjects for teaching. I was told it was difficult verging on impossible to find a mathematics teacher, whereas the History Department could arrange necessary teaching coverage if I shifted. Mathematics, from my earliest studies in grade school, had always been an easy subject for me, and one I liked. I continued it into college, through calculus, and found the homework within my reach. It had been my habit to do my mathematics homework last because, though tired late in the evening, I found it challenging and interesting enough to slug through the work in just a few minutes.

Hence, shortly after arrival, I had begun teaching in the Mathematics Department, having survived the inspection of the head, Dr. Conwell, who provided continuing support and help. As the war months went on, it happened that teaching mathematics at St. Paul's was a good way for me to do my part, in the opinion of the draft board in Cambridge, which had the final say on such things.

Nevertheless, there were moments, of course, when I wondered whether I was doing enough or all that was possible in the national effort. At one of these moments of thoughtful wonder, I remember—it was, I think, in winter 1944–45—writing a letter to "The Pentagon, Washington, D.C." Just who would get this letter I did not stop to worry about. It was my writing of it that was important. In the letter I inquired about the possibility of my undertaking a short service project of some sort that would take me from St. Paul's for a month or two of activity and then deposit me back in Concord for my "real" job. It was certainly a long shot, if not a wild shot. Nothing happened that I could connect with this inquiry.

Then, in March or April 1945, a telegram from some part of the War Department arrived, inquiring about my availability for six months. I thought this too long and replied: interested but cannot do six months. Shortly after—the pace now quickened—I received a telephone call one day after lunch, describing something or other available, and asking, "Could you be at the Pentagon, in Washington, D.C., tomorrow morning at 9 A.M.?" My limitless confidence and sense of invincibility again took over. I said yes. Margie and I put Billy in the hands of friends, then raced off to Boston for the overnight sleeper to Washington. We spent the night in the upper berth together and arrived at the Pentagon at nine the next morning. I distinctly remember not saluting, as I did not know how.

Everyone deserves to be lucky, at least occasionally. We were on this occasion. Margie had been in close touch with friends from Fort Wayne, Indiana, her home, who were married. The husband at this time was posted to the Pentagon, and they had a small apartment in Washington. When we knew in late afternoon that we were going overnight to Washington, Margie called her friends, who said, "Move in with us for the day or two you will be here. It will be tight but we can make do."

We did. The man was a lieutenant, so in addition to providing us a place to stay, he gave me much-needed unofficial advice on what I was undergoing.

In two days I was weighed and measured top to toe—in both a physical sense and in examinations, ending up with orders to report again to the Pentagon in about ten days for a flight to the U.K. Uniforms, raincoat, and gear of sorts were thrust into our hands before we returned to Concord. I remember nothing about the return trip.

In the hurried afternoon before leaving Concord I had checked first with Dr. Conwell, head of the Math Department. Could they spare me for a few weeks (it was then summer, and the army indication was that I would be back in Concord by late August)? Yes. Then on to the rector with this improbable tale. "Can I help you?" Mr. Nash asked. I said, "Yes. Do you know Judge Walton in Cambridge, chair of my draft board?" "Yes. We grew up in Cambridge together." "Could you telephone him about this rather wild activity and get his permission?" "Yes. Done."

Ten days later I was back in Washington. In short order I was transported to Patuxent Naval Air Station and boarded a night flight, with nine others, in a very large bomber assigned for Admiral Ernest King's personal transport (he did not need it that night). We landed in Scotland and then journeyed down to London (we stayed in the Cumberland Hotel at Marble Arch) and endless work at 20 Grosvenor Square (the building where Eisenhower planned the '44 invasion). We also took a flight to Essen, Germany, traveled throughout

Germany and some parts of France, experienced many jeep rides, and ate much cold food. Eventually we returned to 20 Grosvenor (in the center of the square was a huge parking lot and storage depot), where I typed, wrote, and edited material for the U.S. Strategic Bombing Survey. After the report was finalized, I flew back to New York City in August.

I felt at this point that I had done something. But the something seemed mighty small. I do not actually cringe when asked about all of this, but at the same time I have huge doubts about my part. I believe this is natural.

Nevertheless, there it is. I arrived back at St. Paul's and resumed my afternoon walks with Margie and our dog, while pushing Billy in some vehicle or other. School life began again in September.

P.S. In contemplating the improbability of these events, it occurs to me that two elements were responsible for my being tapped for this duty: my Harvard academic degrees and the fact that I could type at eighty-five words a minute with minimal errors. The Pentagon had a personnel problem; it needed an analyst for this assignment, and it needed a typist. Was there a typist who could write copy when needed? Was there an analyst who could type? With me, they got two for one.

—June 30, 2012

One Player Was Missing

In this chapel talk during Lent in 1946, Bill speaks with the passionate firsthand knowledge of one who has seen war's destructive force. In language that sounds surprisingly self-critical of the school in which he was still a very junior teacher, he challenges the privileged sons of his adopted community with a foretaste of the words that his Harvard contemporary, John F. Kennedy, would use to summon the nation fifteen years later: "To what extent do we take everything for granted, believing that all is owed unto us but that we owe nothing in return?" This essay shows that the young mathematics master and budding administrator was already thinking in the broadest terms about the mission of his school, firm in his conviction that it owed the world—and its own best self— more than merely the next generation of partners at J. P. Morgan and Company. He placed striking—even insistent—emphasis on the integral place of the arts in a well-rounded education, and in a well-lived life.

A FOOTBALL GAME was played at the Lower Grounds in late November a few years ago to decide the championship of a series which had been closely contested that fall. It was a cold, gray, cheerless day of the type familiar to us in New Hampshire, a good day for staying indoors, perhaps, but also good for football, especially for a championship game. A player for one of the teams, a strong tackle, did not appear for the game. Knowing that the boy was not in the infirmary or otherwise detained in the school, the coach inquired that evening to discover the reason for his absence, only to find, much to his disappointment, that the player did not like to play football on cold, cheerless days. To know that this boy was one of the most able, intellectually, in his form, and to know that later that same year at graduation this boy won many of the prizes offered, only makes this failure harder to accept.

Five-year old Mary had dressed and gone downstairs upon waking early from her nap. When Mother appeared sometime later, little bits of chocolate cake still clinging to her mouth and cheeks indicated clearly that Mary had had a little snack, although this was against her Mother's instructions. Several casual questions produced no information, nor did her Mother's first direct questions, but finally, under persistent and intense pressure, Mary admitted, "Yes, Mother, I did have a little lunch. I ate a banana."

What is there that is common to both of these experiences? There is, I think, this: an easy, unquestioning acceptance of privileges and advantages, but an inadequate regard for the responsibilities that accompany them. Is there not in each of us a willingness to accept without hesitation the work and attention and devotion and love of others, and at the same time a tendency to be negligent about the accompanying responsibilities?

We are not surprised that a five-year-old girl has failed to learn the inexorable demands of honesty. Her respect for truth will grow with added experience and time, first through fear of punishment, later by coming to understand that in the long run a truthful policy is more expedient; and finally she will act honestly because of moral principle.

More serious, however, is the case of the football player. For here is a seventeen-year-old young man who had shared the comradeship of team practice and play, who had tasted its elation in success and had suffered its discouragement in failure, who, by his voluntary association with the team and by his physical ability and spirit, had taught both teammates and coach to count upon him for help—"Love's best habit is in seeming trust"—only to fail, in time of need, his teammates, his coach, and also himself. For this boy will never be proud of himself "when to the sessions of sweet silent thought [he] summon[s] up remembrance of things past."

What is the meaning of the word "responsibility"? Literally, to respond with something. The Latin word *respondere*, from which our word responsibility has come, meant to answer to when used by Cicero and Livy, but its earlier and more pure use by Plautus had the definite meaning of promising something in return. It is in this sense that I like to think of the word responsibility, that in enjoying certain privileges and opportunities, we promise something in return.

Why do we so often fail to respond adequately to our responsibilities? Three reasons, among many, will serve my purposes: first, that we do not think at all, that the idea of something owed in return does not enter our minds; second, if we do think a little, we do not think clearly; and third, when we recognize clearly what we ought to do, we often refuse to do it, willfully and with a knowing mind. Each of these reasons should be explained further.

Do we think at all of our responsibilities in many aspects of our school life? To what extent do we take everything for granted, believing that all is owed unto us but that we owe nothing in return?

There are two types of waiters in the dining halls of our school. The first, when asked to go to the kitchen to get something, will always answer, "But it is John's turn," John being the other waiter that week; whereas the second type of waiter will go quickly and silently to accomplish the task. The first boy believes that the most important thing in the world is that the chores connected with waiting tables should be divided with mathematical precision between the two unfortunate wretches who happen to be serving time; he does not mind that his attitude is thoughtless, selfish, and self-indulgent, for he believes, with Lady Macbeth, that "A little water clears us of this deed."

The second boy is wiser, and in his greater wisdom knows that in the long run work will be divided evenly, if that be a consideration at all. But further he realizes that in a world wracked in confusion and turmoil, where thousands lack the daily necessities of life, the least ounce of realization of responsibility by any one of us who enjoys such favored treatment as we have here requires that we promise something in return, in this case a ready willingness to help in the small way requested of us and to do this in a manner that will make life as pleasant as possible for everyone concerned. Having reached a thoughtful decision and resolutely determined upon a course of action, he is no "pipe for Fortune's finger to sound what stop she please."

How often do our actions indicate that, without adequate thought, we enjoy the soft belief that everything belongs to us, that we must promise nothing in return?

If failure to think at all is one explanation of our inattention to our responsibilities, failure to think clearly is certainly a second explanation. How often do we allow petty considerations or feelings to mar important decisions; how much do we mix our motives; how much do we rationalize a desired action into a right action?

Sunday evenings, after evensong, each of us has the opportunity of hearing expressions of the genius of man as they have come down to us in magnificent organ music, so magnificently played; the opportunity of hearing music in a chapel without the feeling of hypocrisy which Pope had in mind when he wrote: "As some to church repair, Not for the doctrine, but the music there." Yet only a few attend. What is music? runs the thought of the typical student here. Well, yes, it is something. There's the symphony orchestra, the opera, radio, and Victrola, and the rhythm bands which have won such a secure place in our Afro-tribal civilization. But what of music?

I don't know; others pay attention to it, but I've got to finish *Terry and the Pirates* back in my room, or a little Latin (there's no other time to do it), or I must see so-and-so, and, well, here I am back at the house, ready to continue my own personal "chronicle of wasted time." Curious about music as one of the means by which man has expressed his loves and fears, his successes and failures, his beliefs and his unbeliefs?—well, I guess not. We have not taken the trouble to learn that "Music resembles poetry; in each / Are nameless graces which no methods teach, / And which a master-hand alone can reach." Custom, in the form of school rules, places upon us the formal obligation of acquainting ourselves with certain areas of human knowledge and experience. Should we not recognize an even more pressing obligation to acquaint ourselves with the major forms of art?

Should our rejection of music and all forms of art not be based upon something more tangible than confusion of mind and an irresolute spirit? Shakespeare tells us that Julius Caesar decided, at one time during the morning of the fateful Ides of March, not to go to the Senate House, and sent the following message: "And tell them that I will not come today; / Cannot is false, and that I dare not, falser; / I will not come today: tell them so, Decius." How often do we delineate as clearly as Caesar the thoughts of our own minds, if only to ourselves?

A third explanation of our failure to live up to our responsibilities is willful rejection; that is, we recognize our obligations clearly and we understand what we ought to do, but we do not do it. We are too lazy; we are too cowardly; we are too easy with ourselves; we prefer to do something else.

The time schedule of the field team investigating bomb damage, with which I was connected last year, called for us to be in London for one week after the completion of our investigations of cities and factories in Germany and Austria, so that a final, summary report could be written. It was thought that the relatively normal atmosphere of London would afford conditions more conducive to the preparation of our report than any city upon the shattered Continent. A certain Captain Jensen, a former intelligence officer of the Air Corps, was therefore assigned to London six weeks before our expected arrival to make all necessary preparations for us, to rent office space, procure office equipment, typewriters, paper, etc. Upon our arrival, anxious to plunge without delay into our work, we found three small offices in Grosvenor Square filled with tattered bits of equipment: sections of desks unassembled, parts of filing cabinets not put together, five English typewriters which had not been used for six months and as a result were not in working order because England's damp air had rusted vital parts fast in their places. There was no telephone, no lights, no paper, no stationery supplies whatsoever. What a discouraging picture. However, twenty-four hours of persistent, resourceful scrounging, which saw many treasures and souvenirs liberated on the Continent crossing the palms of supply sergeants who were strategically placed, which even saw a small raiding party upon the private paper stock of a general to obtain several reams of bond paper (elsewhere not to be found in the whole European Theater of Operations), and our office was functioning smoothly, for so must things go in the army when there is a deadline on certain work to be done.

But what of Captain Jensen and the six weeks he had had to get things into good working order in advance of our arrival? Captain Jensen, we learned, had arrived at the office punctually at nine o'clock as required and immediately began to read *Stars and Stripes*. An hour or so later came several morning London newspapers, perhaps *Yank*, then a letter to someone back home, a telephone call to his English wife, and, well, it was time for lunch. After lunch came a trip to the PX, perhaps a small errand to be run for the office, and so went the day. There is no question that Captain Jensen understood clearly his responsibilities. Our conclusion was that he willfully refused to face them. Hamlet said it this way: "Sure, he that made us with such large discourse / Looking before and after, gave us not / That capability and god-like reason / To fust in us unused."

Our abilities and our reason must not mold for lack of use. Freedom of action we have today, but should we not question seriously whether this freedom is expansive enough to allow us to turn willfully from the use of our abilities which reason dictates? If we do shrink from our responsibilities, unhappiness will be our lot, and we would "better be with the dead . . . than on the torture of the mind to lie in restless ecstasy."

How often do we in this place fail to think at all of our responsibilities in different situations, or fail to think about them clearly; or if we do understand our obligations, how often do we turn from them knowingly and refuse to accept our heritage?

How much responsibility do we recognize toward Christianity? Yes, we go to sacred studies classes, we prepare

26

assignments, we come to chapel, but this meets only the bare requirements. Do we recognize a responsibility for active participation, do we anxiously seek the richness of the experiences that can be ours, do we seek help for others, in the infinite resources of our common religion?

How much responsibility do we feel toward our studies, beyond the preparation of the assignment for the next day? How much do we share the writer's experiences when we read the great classics of our language?

How much do we thrill at the relentless logic of the human mind as expressed in plane geometry (or is it mostly a collection of unfathomable theoretical principles and intricate problems)? How many of us nowadays stride beyond the terrors of the ablative absolute to the soft delicacy of the love poems of Catullus?

We clean our rooms daily in the period between breakfast and chapel; how much responsibility do we take during the rest of any day for the cleanliness of our school? Discarded newspapers and assorted trash line the halls of our dormitories and sometimes our paths and lawns, because no one has time (or is it no one has the mind?) to feel responsible for the appearance of things, and this is so even though trash be piled high outside our own room door.

The obligation to recognize responsibility, to recognize it clearly, and then to assume it and do something about it—how often are these lacking?

There is no more significant fact in this country today, though it be a negative fact, than the failure of citizens to take an active part in government. By this is not meant, of course, that more people should run for senator or governor or dog catcher, but that we as citizens should be more politically conscious, more politically awake, and more politically active. That we should recognize clearly the obligations that accompany citizenship, that we should shoulder some of the responsibilities of political government. Aristotle said that man is a political animal; but in our civilization he has gone to sleep. Now sleep may "knit up the ravell'd sleave of care," but if we sleep too long today, we may never awaken; the whole garment may have been destroyed. There is no question but that we are enjoying to the full the privileges of citizenship, privileges which today set off the citizen of this country as the most favored person on earth.

What of the responsibilities of citizenship which accompany these privileges? Has any one of us performed a political act since the time of the last election? Or do we think that political acts are the exclusive province of the professional politician? (If so, how wrong we are.) How easy it is to criticize the difficulties of our government today; but how much have we helped to find the right solution? It is not the responsibility of "those politicians," it is our responsibility, yours and mine. For this is a representative government as well as a government by representatives; we face the inescapable obligation of helping keep our representatives informed of what we think should be done, in addition to the obligation of voting for the best qualified man at election time. Washington does care. Washington is a big ear tuned to the ground, anxious to know what the people want. Recent proof, if needed, can be found in the backing given Mr. Bowles by the little people in his victory, or partial victory, against the spirals of inflationary destruction. [Chester Bowles recently had been named to head the federal Office of Economic Stabilization.]

How much time is there? To Milton, writing at the age of twenty-three, time was the "suttle theef of youth." How much danger is there, in our age, that time will be the subtle thief of civilization? Who among us is perfectly confident that there will be a civilized world, such as we know it now at least, still in existence five years from tonight, in the face of the destructive possibilities of atomic energy? Yet who among us has done one single solitary thing about it? How negligent we are of our responsibilities as citizens, even when we are prodded by self-interest. Can we not muster more than the "soft phrases of peace" to oppose what Othello called "the tyrant custom," maker of war? Can we produce a responsive citizenry, thankful for its many privileges and alert to its many responsibilities?

How many graduates of this school look forward to a life of service to the public? There should be more than there are. Should not a political life be held in greater esteem? Perhaps the most important result of Franklin Roosevelt's attack upon big business in the 1930s will prove to be that, insofar as the prospect of unlimited monetary reward in business has been checked, to that extent has the relative attractiveness of public service been increased. We strive to increase the sale of Wheaties; should we not strive just as vigorously to improve our government? We hear that it is occasionally necessary for the State Department to announce that not all of its important members are graduates of the Groton School; would that it were necessary someday for someone to announce that not all governors or senators, or even police judges, were graduates of this school.

Yes, just as it is the obligation of the citizen to consider carefully the ways by which he can contribute to the effectiveness of the operation of our government for 364 days a year, in addition to Election Day, so too is it the obligation and the privilege of the young person to consider carefully the opportunities and merits of public service.

The great challenge which faces us today is to be faithful to our responsibilities. From our minds we must require a clear recognition of the meaning of our responsibilities; from our hearts we must hope for and expect the resolution to fulfill the same. And if this conception of our responsibilities leads us down a hard and difficult road, we do not need go far for comfort and example. For in the life of Jesus Christ, and particularly in his days of torment and death which we honor and cherish in these weeks of remembrance, we can find sources of consolation and encouragement which are equal to our most difficult trials.

Tempted often to dilute his conception of his mission and his responsibilities, Jesus met his greatest temptation at the end when he was offered his life in exchange for a compromise with principle. "He saved others; let him save himself." "If thou be the king of the Jews, save thyself." Clear, bold, courageous was the answer which we all know: "Father, forgive them; for they know not what they do." So in his life, so in his death we can find strength, example, and devotion to help us meet with greater confidence our challenge: to recognize clearly and to meet faithfully the responsibilities that are ours.

Realizing that "the flighty purpose never is o'ertook," can we resolve that "from this moment the very firstlings of [our] hearts shall be the firstlings of [our] hands"?

—Chapel, 1946

Why Stop Learning?

In this undated talk to a Concord civic group in the late 1940s, Bill reflects on challenges that the rapid changes of the postwar world would pose for an educated and informed citizenry. He cites his own personal journey of learning and experience, but his perspective suggests an early awareness of the ways in which American institutions—including, one can only assume, St. Paul's—would have to adapt to keep pace with new realities. His global perspective is coupled with a call for local action. His words about the duties inherent in a democratic society ring true with surprising force and prescience in today's hyperpartisan political environment—and the often ill-informed political debates of the twenty-first century.

TWO CONFESSIONS must be presented to you at the outset. Firstly, that the phrase "Why Stop Learning?" was cribbed in toto from Dorothy Canfield Fisher, being the title of a book published in 1927, one of the first, incidentally, to attempt to publicize and popularize the subject of adult education. And secondly, I am forced, in all candor, to parade my lack of qualifications to answer this question. I am just a plain teacher; perhaps, however, an atypical teacher in that I studied ancient history and Latin literature as an undergraduate, Roman history and literature for one year in Germany before the latest war, and modern European history in graduate school in this country, and I teach mathematics. Lest someone have serious doubts about the type of mathematics teaching in my school, let me add, hurriedly, that I had two years of college mathematics, through calculus, following out my interest in the subject.

When one looks at education in the modern world, whether here in this country or abroad, one is immediately struck by the amount and the profundity of the reverence which is showered upon the attainment of a degree or a diploma or some such handle—which indicates that a certain amount of time has been spent and presumes that certain things have been accomplished. One young man of my acquaintance, whose college years were interrupted by service in the army, felt upon his discharge that he was ready to enter the business world. But during his first months in business for himself (his energy and initiative took him to South America, where he was active in the disposal of surplus government property), he so frequently encountered the questions "What about your degree?" or "Have you finished college?" that he acquired thereby a knowledge of the obeisance of the modern world to the symbol. I now address my letters to him in care of Harvard College, where he is struggling with English 23 and Philosophy 8b—at least until September 3, when he becomes a free man.

But I am not here concerned with an evaluation of this situation, knowing that a systematic and effective defense could be made for the system, and that many positive influences and advantages result from it, as well as disadvantages. Rather am I here interested in pointing out the effect of the system on the attitude toward learning held by the average American. You go through the paces. You learn something, perhaps. You pursue the symbol. You achieve the symbol. Period. The time of education is past. The stamp of something or other has been placed upon you, and there is no further need to think, question, or learn.

That this position is fundamentally false seems to me to require no argument. That it is also inordinately wasteful, unfortunate, unnecessary, and positively dangerous, in the modern world, is what I wish now to discuss.

Formal education comes to an end, whether at fourteen, eighteen, twenty-two, or at twenty-five, before the young person has had the opportunity of seeing much of life or of enjoying a great many diverse experiences. Necessarily then, in many fields such as politics, religion, economics, history, and others, he has studied topics as symbols, without knowing at firsthand their true meaning. Certainly the young student cannot be compared in background and experience with an older person who has encountered the impact of some of these forces in his own life.

May I cite a personal example to illustrate my point? As a freshman in college, I read the *Agricola*, written by Tacitus about A.D. 93, a short biographical sketch of his father-in-law, a man who had been a famous leader of the Roman legions. This short book contains a passage, my memory of which to this day is sharp and clear, as is still the reaction I had to it then: what a hate had Tacitus for Domitian! Domitian, you may recall, was one of the first of the Roman emperors to use his arbitrary power despotically and frequently to the consequent total loss of freedom in Rome, as Tacitus testifies. My initial and only impression at that time concerned the personal feeling of Tacitus toward Domitian: Tacitus hated Domitian. Needless to say, when I came upon this passage a few weeks ago, in English translation in a book I was reading, my reaction was totally different. My first thought was, yes, it was hell in the ancient world to be without political freedom, as it was so recently in most of Western Europe and is still today in the part of the world controlled by the USSR. The personal experiences I had had since that freshman class had so nurtured my power to understand that a whole wealth of new meaning came to me from the same words.

One can say, I think with some confidence, that there are vast areas of learning which cannot be accurately comprehended by the immature student, and it is, then, only to the degree that mature minds question, study, and learn, whether informally by themselves or in groups, that genuine progress can be made in these fields.

But of what importance is it, you may ask, that men and women in the modern world continue to question and learn in their adult lives? Do they not learn enough in formal education to last them through their lives?

It is clear that the world in modern times has been shaken repeatedly by a series of revolutions—industrial, technological, managerial, political, scientific—and by the holocaust of war. Age-old as the phrase is, times have changed, but age-old also is its truth, The old ideas and patterns of thought are not necessarily the correct ones today, whether what one has learned is one year old or thirty. (I do not, of course, argue that the old, ipso facto, is untrue, but rather that it is often untrue and that a questioning spirit is required.)

I remember vividly what a shock it was to me ten or twelve years ago to discuss with my father the subject of the national tariff. Fresh out of courses in economics and modern history, I was converted to the new, yet harsh facts of modern life wherein international cooperation was held a better and more worthwhile goal than the maintenance of a rigid national sovereignty and the determination of what was best for the predominant local pressure group. My father had not studied history, law, or economics formally for twenty-five years, and was a typical Midwesterner in his fanatic devotion to the old. We've now had a war. Would the events of the past decade have been different if, in the Midwest alone, there had existed a questioning, searching turn of mind during the past half century, perhaps guided by community forums and discussion groups, intelligently led—instead of the pat yet violent acceptance of things as they had been learned years ago?

Have we realized yet as a nation the full implications of the political revolution which has come to its full fruition only in the past generation? I am referring to the change from representative government to democratic government. Our Constitution was written with the intention that the ordinary citizen would not participate in the details of government. He would, rather, elect the best men he could to the government, and those men would in turn do their best in their places of responsibility. An elected official, in the early years of our country, thought little of the particular interests of his electorate and much of the general interests of the country. Now, with the individual income tax as a political weapon and football, with the direct election of senators and all other important public servants, with the development of mass media in communication making it possible for the individual to be articulate and influential in the details of government, as well as in the election of the governors—with these and other changes having taken place, we are confronted with a situation wherein the role the individual is called upon to play has assumed importance greater than ever before.

Can we afford to allow the economics of the voter to be thirty years out of date? Can we be content when outdated and untrue historical generalities are in current and extensive circulation? A little-known incident from the recent war will illustrate the important function of the average citizen of our country. Germany, in September 1940, stood in the full flush of victory, Western Europe at her knees, with the exception of England, which was expected to come to terms shortly. America was not in the war, Russia was an ally. Hitler and the little group which ran Germany, confident that the war was over or nearly so, decided that they could finish up with the weapons they then possessed, if they could have them in sufficient quantities. They therefore ordered fundamental research on radar to cease and directed the engineering skill of the German nation to the mass production of models then in existence.

This decision was not revoked until the summer of 1942, nearly two years later, when it had become clear that, after all, the war was not over, that Russia was a formidable opponent, and that America was going to make its influence felt. What happened in our country and in England? Here, no single man had the power to make such an important decision singly. Rather, a committee of scientists had complete charge of the allocation of materials, money, and time to various projects, but their decisions were based solely upon their best estimate of what science could accomplish, of what appeared most promising for future work. Amid the pull and haul, checks and counterbalances of a democracy, even a democracy fighting for its life, fundamental research on radar proceeded without interruption. And what was the result? At the invasion of Normandy in June 1944, the Allies enjoyed complete radar control of the operation. Every German radar station on the entire Atlantic coast was blacked out. Allied radar operated without hindrance, charting every important German movement. A time lag of two years in fundamental research on radar had placed Germany irretrievably behind in the race for perfection.

If such is the power of the demos, the people, in our democracy, should we not be concerned with the opinions and thought processes of those same people? Can we afford to comfort ourselves with the complacent thought that because it all worked out well once, it will again? Is not the essence of democracy that it depends upon the stirrings of the people themselves for its strength?

Consider for a moment the impact of the modern revolutions upon the individual. He works eight hours a day, five days a week. Think of the time at his disposal: how is it to be used? It is a matter of historical record that the Wesleyan ministers and other reformers (I was born and raised a Methodist in the English tradition, so I am here casting no partisan stones) labored valiantly and hard, in the late eighteenth century and in the nineteenth century, to lead the working groups away from their slavish addiction to gin, from the sordidness of their lives to a more lofty level of group morality, but without as much success as was achieved in the twinkling of an eye at the beginning of this century with the introduction on a vast scale of the cinema as a form of entertainment, and with the new availability to the working man of a means of transportation, the bicycle, which allowed him to tour the countryside in his free time. We regret the influence of the cinema upon the morality of our world today without having at the same time an awareness of its tremendous influence for good in the past. But that much is history.

The next step is of course elsewhere, and if the giant strides taken in the modern world in the past generation, which have given us undreamed-of leisure hours, are not to go down for no purpose, we must see to it that some worthwhile and satisfying gains are recorded.

The modern revolutions have brought their problems in the complexities of society, but they have also brought with them the means of survival: leisure hours. Can these moments be harnessed to a useful purpose? Can the average citizen come to desire to employ some of this free time for significant purposes?

In all fairness it must be admitted, of course, that much is being done. Every fraternal and social organization in Concord, I dare say, has its "educational committee," some dead as the worst in education, some as alive and constructive as the best. Groups exist in Concord and elsewhere, by themselves and without affiliation of any kind, wherein the sole devotion is to the questioning spirit and to the desire for knowing. Certainly the educational influence of your organization, the Consumer Cooperative, has been in the right direction, to say nothing of its economic or other influences.

But it would be a rash man, indeed, who would confess himself satisfied. More can be done. Some of the men of St. Paul's School are currently engaged in trying to establish some sort of study center for this community, which would offer courses of study in specific fields for a period of eight or ten weeks a year, with classes meeting an hour or so a week. More can be done and should be done, and our good wishes and backing should attend every effort in this direction.

— *Concord, late 1940s*

The Sanctuary

In the late 1960s, as he pursued doctoral work at Harvard, Bill was asked to join the board of the Sanctuary, an organization of Harvard College established to provide help to troubled people who flocked to Harvard Square from the Boston area. The Sanctuary received financial support and the use of Harvard buildings. The board employed paid counselors from the Harvard graduate schools. Reflecting the helping culture current among attitudes and theories of the graduate schools, the board and the counselors labored evenings to help people caught in the swirling activist attitudes of the time. As rector, Bill brought counselors and facilitators from the Sanctuary to St. Paul's to help bridge the same gap in attitudes that was spreading throughout the country. These sessions helped set the tone for discussions of changes in community attitudes. Bill wrote this essay years later as a reminiscence.

THE SANCTUARY sponsored and monitored a number of immensely important activities in and around Harvard Square, starting about 1968 and continuing through the middle 1970s, to the benefit of the local community, Harvard College, and the greater Boston area.

Harvard Square has long been an attractive beacon for the young and curious, those probing normal social limits. It still is. Harvard Square had a heightened attractiveness in those years, bringing waves of fragile young people and activist challengers of all stripes to this dynamic bit of real estate almost beyond compare. But these antisocial behaviors included fighting, which could get out of hand; abusive conduct by one person to another, often directed toward the younger and less experienced, possibly inflicting psychological and developmental wounds; and crowd activities that moved beyond accepted civil limits. Isolated examples of these activities were appearing throughout the country and could be expected to increase nationally as long as raw divisions and cracks in the national discourse continued.

The establishment and development of the Sanctuary and its support by Harvard College owed much to one remarkable young Harvard administrator, John Marquand. John arrived at Harvard in the early 1960s as a graduate student in history, after graduating from Wesleyan, where he had been an outstanding student and college leader. He was president of the student government and of his class in his senior year. Following several years of outstanding graduate work, he became a teaching assistant in the History Department and had a series of important Harvard College administrative positions. In the late 1960s he was senior tutor of Lowell House and a member of the Administrative Board of Harvard College. He became widely known for his intelligent interest in student affairs and his unstinting help to the young, naturally resulting in his leadership of the Sanctuary.

The Sanctuary had a board of directors of six to eight people, quietly established by Harvard College. The college committed $350,000 to $400,000 annually. Harvard also located and assigned to the Sanctuary space in college buildings, primarily buildings on Mount Auburn Street near the subway entrance in the square. The Sanctuary board at this time included John Marquand as chairman; the rectors of several Boston Episcopal churches; the dean of the Episcopal Theological Seminary; three senior members of the Faculty of Arts and Sciences; David Bynum Jr., an Episcopal priest, as staff director; and myself. All were known for their professional work and also for a desire to understand youth and the current street scene. The board met most Thursday evenings at the home of the dean of the seminary. Close, informal liaison with the college on plans and activities was established and maintained by Bob Tonis, a fine professional and the chief of the Harvard University Police, known for his sympathy and understanding combined with a secure sense of his responsibilities.

Almost all the physical activities of the Sanctuary were centered on the general Harvard Square area during the evenings, 6 P.M. through 11 P.M., continuing lightly to 2 or 3 A.M. On a typical evening there would be five to eight graduate students walking, sitting, talking, and listening in the square. Most of the Sanctuary's work was supported by the careful efforts of students in the Graduate School of Education counseling program and the Psychology Department of the Faculty of Arts and Sciences.

A passing observer walking through the square would not have been able to identify the graduate students. Their normal dress at classes and in libraries, and while performing their paid work evenings in the square, was the standard dress of graduate students of the day. Their usual appearance: bib overalls (somewhat disheveled), long hair, and a confident look that there was nothing more important in life than continued informal discussion of the problems of humankind and modern citizen states. This offhand appearance was a necessary part of the counselors' task: to spot possible trouble, to hang close and gradually participate and monitor developments, seeking help from police and others when necessary.

The "classic" case: during the evening, a girl, perhaps fifteen years old, would become the object of attention by another person. Observing this, the Sanctuary representative would ask, "Do you know where you are going to spend the night?" Answer: "No, and I don't care." "How about phoning your mother and father, asking that they come for you?" "No. Never. I never want to see them again." In time the girl might feel comfortable enough to accept the Sanctuary counselor's suggestion of a warm and safe place to stay, and they would walk to the Sanctuary's headquarters on Mount Auburn Street. (This space housed a dormitory with twenty beds for women and girls, as well as twenty beds for men and boys.) After being greeted by an older woman, the girl would eagerly eat what was offered, perhaps have a shower, and then go to bed. The following morning, counselors would continue their efforts to find a way for her to return comfortably to family or friends. These efforts were limited by law to seventy-two hours and occasionally led to a disappointing outcome.

I cite this example as a way of showing the effectiveness of the counselors in their role as helpers to people in trouble. Early in such discussions, it was crucial to establish a relationship of trust. The counselors' stated position: we will take no action whatsoever in addition to talking with you without your full and informed willingness.

Close cooperation among Bob Tonis, his Harvard officers, the chief of the Cambridge Police Department and his officers, and Sanctuary personnel was essential. This cooperation was managed carefully by all sides and met an important need when passing on general information to Cambridge officials who had broader responsibilities. Thus, through the labors of many people, street life in Harvard Square was maintained throughout this period within acceptable bounds.

The discussions and considerations in board meetings were challenging, enlightening, and instructive. In November 1972, with the permission of the Sanctuary board, six counselors, Harvard graduate students, were invited to St. Paul's for the weekend. When I introduced them, I stated my objective for the visit: help for anyone at the school, student or faculty, which could come through conversation with our guests. The six arrived toward the end of lunch on Friday and began conversations that lasted throughout the afternoon, through dinner, and into the evening. The principal "offices" for the counselors were the Upper dining halls.

When I invited the counselors to visit, I asked that there be no reports back to me. And I cautioned the visiting counselors not to use names and not to seek names from those who talked with them. I explained this objective to the school. Anonymity was the word. My wish was to facilitate discussions.

It was no surprise for me to hear, unofficially, that the first hours of these discussions were testing periods. Was this visit real, in the way it had been described by the rector? He had no agenda? Come on! The counselors established their trust, however, within an hour or two of their arrival, and subsequently they were mobbed.

I enjoyed my work with the board of the Sanctuary. It was through Zeph Stewart, master of Lowell House, a good friend, that I first met John Marquand. I saw John frequently in 1966–67, my sabbatical year of residence at Harvard, and had several opportunities during this period to note directly his single-minded devotion to quietly helping others. He seemed to live for such opportunities. John resigned from the board about 1970, to be followed as chairman by Harvey Guthrie, dean of the Episcopal Theological Seminary.

P.S. Board meetings usually ran from 7 to 9 P.M. on Thursdays. George Trippe, an SPS employee, would pick me up at 5:30 after a normal busy day and quick supper, drive me to Cambridge, and then drive me back. I had one of the school's station wagons fitted with a board and mattress contraption that could be placed in the rear with the back seats removed. Emerging from the meeting, I would get in the back and sleep all the way to Concord, where George waked me to transfer, quietly, to the rectory. Board meeting attended. Maximum rest achieved. All went well.

—July 7, 2012

Part Two

TAKING·CHARGE

Traditions and Changes

As Bill took the helm of the school in the spring of 1970, he struck an exquisite balance between honoring long-standing traditions and engineering swift change. His first move—even before the trustees voted on May 1 to begin admitting girls as soon as practicable—was to eliminate compulsory attendance at two Sunday chapel services (a decision announced before Matt Warren's official retirement). He knew, as he would put it in his first annual report, that in such tumultuous times "it is exceedingly important for St. Paul's School to maintain emphasis on enduring values," but also to change and, "as appropriate, lead in change." In this passage from his first Rector's Letter in the Alumni Horae, *he takes note of the daunting task ahead of him, with an affectionate nod to the intense feelings of the young men now in his care.*

DEAR ALUMNI: Nature is benevolent and kindly in late May and June in Millville, which is the principal reason Anniversary was changed in 1864 from St. Paul's Day in January to the latter part of the spring, according to a history of the early days of the School. Weather was of particular importance this year because the weekend saw not only the traditional activities of

Anniversary but, for the first time, the Graduation of the Sixth Form as well. Sixth Formers and their families, and the School, heard a remarkable address by Prof. E. Dudley H. Johnson, '30, Chairman of the Princeton English Department, on Sunday afternoon, May 31st, as the culminating point of three busy days. The weather was cloudless and nearly perfect during the entire weekend.

This season brings the fulfillment of ancient School customs—Shattucks and Halcyons rowing in vigorous and spirited competition; the Flag Pole ceremonies and the awarding of medals and cups (and now kisses, a tradition established by Malcolm Kenneth Gordon); the Saturday evening dinners of reunioning forms—each important in itself and as part of customs long honored by graduates and members of the School.

And yet, in the celebrations enjoyed by all, our activities momentarily masked the deep concerns we feel for the heavy pressures under which young men live out their youth. Who can fully appreciate the contradictions and conflicts which flow from the variety of roles that a St. Paul's student must fulfill? The expectations of housemaster, teacher, coach, headmaster, and parents paint a vivid background for what has always been an arena of momentous conflict. In this conflict choices must be made between the expectations of society and the current revisions of these expectations expressed by the young. In all probability there is less overlap now between these two worlds, and at the same time a stronger attraction exercised by the new cultural patterns, than ever before.

Parents and schoolmasters, better than others, have known through the ages the many meanings of tolerance. We stretch toward charity and compassion, those greatest of virtues, as we continue to try to appreciate and understand the several worlds inhabited simultaneously by each young person, and as we seek with the splendid young men of the School to learn how to live acceptably if not comfortably with the ambiguities of our world.

Thank you for your understanding, stated so frequently in letters and calls and visits. And thank you, too, for the remarkable help expressed in the Alumni and Parents Funds, and in so many other ways. As our country needs the fine young graduates of our School, so we continue to need your interest and attention. We are most grateful to you for your support.

—*Rector's Letter, Summer 1970*

The Dress Code

Not every decision Bill faced in these crowded years was momentous. But, St. Paul's being the insular world it was, even the smallest matters could loom large in the school's psyche. In this chapel talk about the SPS dress code—or, rather, the sudden lack of one—Bill shows that he was not without a sense of humor. In my student days, the maxim "nice slacks are nice" was the law of the land for girls' trousers, and not just in winter. The guidelines set forth here endure, more or less, to this day, which may well be seen as proof of their wisdom and as a teaching opportunity outside the classroom.

I WANT TO TALK with you this morning about clothes, your dress here at school for classes, chapel, and cafeteria meals.

You will remember—those of you who were here last spring—my announcement at the Last Night program in Memorial Hall that there would be a change in clothes starting in September. I said ties, jackets, skirts, and dresses would no longer be required at chapel, classes, and cafeteria meals. Rather, we would adopt a standard for clothes described in the words "neat, clean, in good repair." No athletic clothes. These characteristics transcend fashion and taste, and express our belief that the way we look is a matter of some significance to us individually, and as a school.

This fall people have not been able to agree readily on the meaning of these words. Some people have had no difficulty in understanding, while I am told other people regard these words as broad, general, imprecise, and subject to misinterpretation.

I would like to suggest that the confusion has arisen from two different ways of looking at the entire announcement about clothes, and not from the words "neat, clean, good repair," and any precision or lack of precision inherent in this phrase. Some people have looked at the general announcement as a whole and have found meaning.

Some people have looked at the specific words for guidance, and in specific interpretation of a short, general phrase have found confusion. The second approach is doomed to failure. Four words will not give precise guidance to almost five hundred people except in situations of extreme simplicity and considerable importance. In a crowded movie house, two words—"Fire, Run!"—will have quite a social impact.

But the subject of clothes has never been renowned for simplicity. Qualities of color, materials, texture, and shape make fashion an endlessly fascinating and diverting concern for many members of the human race.

No, we cannot expect precise guidance from these four words.

But looking at the general announcement as a whole, in the context of life here at school and in our country, I think there is clear meaning, and I think this clear meaning is self-evident for the entire community.

We have dropped the formalism of an earlier era. We have introduced the informal atmosphere characteristic of present life in America. That, I think, is the simple message of this change.

This change, from formality to informality in dress, has occurred throughout our country. Businessmen who once went to work in dark blue suits, white shirts, and bowler hats, now wear bright checks, shirts of many colors, and ties of breadth, color, and design that dazzle and challenge Christmas shoppers. The religious of the Roman Catholic church, leaving their traditional commitment to education and hospitals, have shed their somber clothes as they have entered more active vocations.

The list is endless. But the essential message is the same, and simple. Formalism has given way to informalism.

I had hoped that we as a school could live with informalism, that clothes would be in good repair, and that we would all continue to be neat and clean. Informal, yes, but also neat and clean.

In my judgment, most of the school began this term with a sensitive regard for these considerations. Many of the school have continued throughout the entire term to show that they understood the message. Unhappily, some among us have not acted in ways consistent with this change, and in my judgment this number has increased as the term has gone along.

I have concluded that the school needs a few specific pieces of advice about clothes. What I shall say now will become applicable at the start of the Winter Term.

In the first place, I hope that this discussion will help the school. Let us continue to look at the general nature of the change we have made in school dress for guidance. Let us dress in happy informalism, remembering the extent of our liberation from the inherited formalism of earlier years.

Neat, clean, in good repair: these continue as the important guiding words for our clothes.

I am going to ask you not to wear blue jeans or bib overalls or jump suits. I want boys to have a shirt of some kind that has a collar of some kind. Turtlenecks are satisfactory in this regard for informal wear, but not at seated meals. For the Winter Term, because of the cold weather, girls may wear nice slacks. You may wonder what "nice" slacks are. I am about to make a profound statement, in answer. The difference between nice slacks and other slacks is that nice slacks are nice. End of profound statement.

For seated meals, we shall continue with tie and jacket; for girls, skirts, dresses, pants suits, or nice slacks.

With these specifics added, I doubt that we shall move from a situation of confusion to one of clarity. Will further specifics need to be added in the future? I would hope not. What I do think is that we as a school need the additional advice that these few specifics provide.

We shall have to continue to rely on the general understanding of the meaning of our change in clothes for most of the guidance that we need. I would urge you to respond to the general nature of the change.

We still are left with something short of complete clarity. We continue to have to live with an ambiguous situation. This is not a source of regret. Many significant human situations cannot be defined with precision. In fact, most of life's treasures are ambiguous. Learning to live with ambiguity is one of the important learnings for all students, and refining the capacity to deal with ambiguity is a never-ending task for adults.

Living in situations where expectations are sharply and clearly defined is relatively easy and mindless. The capacity to tolerate ambiguous situations happily and healthily, however, is something that must be learned with practice.

Furthermore, each of us is changing every day, and hence our school is changing. Specifics can apply most appropriately only to a given moment in time, and they tend to hold us back therefore from our drive to develop and change, and become. One of Carl Rogers's books has the arresting title, *On Becoming a Person*. His belief is that each of us is in the constant stage of becoming—becoming more fulfilled to our individual promise as people.

We need fluidity, I think. We need ambiguity. We need the chance to change and to develop. And therefore we should have the absolute minimum of specifics in our relationships.

Have a good vacation. You will return from your mothers neat, clean, and in good repair. I hope we can all struggle hard to stay that way.

—Chapel, December 13, 1971

First Chapel with Girls

The trustees' decision to begin coeducation was effectively coterminous with Bill's election as rector, and the orderly admission of girls was his first great administrative challenge. The first full-time female contingent of nineteen souls arrived in Millville in January 1971, among them a descendant of one of the school's earliest trustees. In this chapel talk from that time, Bill related the school's latest experiment to the currents of change abroad in the land.

WELCOME TO EVERYONE. Welcome to the girls who are here with us this morning for the first time. Welcome back to all of us old-timers. Welcome even for this one morning to those who have not arrived on time.

Monday evening, as you may have heard, the girls who entered the school that day gathered in the Old Chapel with many of us for a brief service, following the custom that is now more than a hundred and ten years old: starting life in this school in that ancient and lovely building.

Today we meet together as a school for the first time, a remarkable moment certainly for all of us as individuals, a historic time for the school as an institution.

What kind of an era are we beginning? What will be the significant developments, the novel characteristics, the unanticipated influences and results?

Vermont Royster, the famous editor of the *Wall Street Journal*, writing yesterday in his column in that paper, speaks of the "conceit" of historians who have taken it upon themselves to tag periods of the past with names: the Dark Ages, the Age of Reason, the Age of Faith, the Roaring Twenties. Royster states, "If most people in the seventeenth and eighteenth centuries were really pretty unenlightened, it is still true that Voltaire, Locke, Hume, and Kant gave the era a different stamp from, say, the eighth century."

Probably the descriptive term the "Age of the Enlightenment" coveys some elements of truth.

Do you know the term "microfiche" or "supermicrofiche"? The general scientific principle of miniaturization, the best-known example of which is the transistor used in radios and television, photography, and high-reduction photography, makes it possible to photograph materials at tremendous reductions in size onto a transparent card called a microfiche. Using the current generation of the microfiche, the supermicrofiche, it is possible to place images of one thousand pages of printed material on a card of the size three inches by five inches.

To view a single page of the thousand on such a card, one can use a reader which throws the page on a screen larger than the original page size, perhaps nine by twelve inches. If, after scanning a page, one wants a copy, this can be obtained through use of a hard-copy printer.

The essentials of this process are compact storage, easy access for research, and the preparation of hard copy of any desired section.

Gradually in the coming years, as funds make possible, this information storage and retrieval process will supplement and perhaps replace the conventional library we know. The *New York Times* plans to have a system such as this in operation by the summer of 1971, this coming summer, embracing all of the information in its own files. This data bank will have editorial materials and news from the daily editions of the *Times*, selections of materials from sixty other newspapers and periodicals, as well as information currently stored in its library. Remarkably, the *Times* plans to make this information available to the general public at its own office and with lesser power at computer consoles throughout the metropolitan area. IBM computers will control access to microfiche storage, and there will be both video screen reproduction for quick viewing and hard-copy printer terminals.

It is not by accident that I have chosen books and periodicals, essential materials of a school, to illustrate what we all are familiar with: the rapid surge of developments in the technological fields which characterize the age in which we live. And which characterize the environment of this school as we celebrate this momentous day in the life of all of us. But extremism also characterizes our country and our age: extremism of both political persuasions, extremism of the left and extremism of the right.

What is extremism? Lipset and Raab, in their newly published book, *The Politics of Unreason*, define extremism as an ideology of moralism, and conspiracy theory, with specific targets of opposition and repression. I quote: "Extremists are those who repudiate the democratic process by denying the legitimacy of political pluralism and the open competition of diverse views. They would confine the marketplace of ideas and interests to those who share their truth ... or who are subject to honest error, but would exclude those whom they charge with evil intentions. The extremists' truth is rigid and absolute. Complex phenomena are treated in terms of single causes and remedies. The driving force in history is the conflict between the extremists' version of good and evil."

To put this in personal and human terms, which I know we can understand more easily, an extremist is one who attempts to relieve his own doubts about his own worth as a person by denying the worth and the humanity of others. Yes, sad to say, extremism characterizes our age as well as technological advance. And perhaps the two are related.

At any rate, following Mr. Royster, we certainly could not say that this primarily is an Age of Technology. And I hope we do not have to admit that the dominant theme of our day compels us to call this the Age of Extremism.

Can we then combine these themes as we search for help and guidance for ourselves, and for this school, as we begin this new epoch? I think we can, at least in the symbolic sense, to which we are limited in such a discussion.

I would suggest that the idea of extremism establishes the problem, and the idea of technology suggests the means by which we can work.

Certainly there are many problems in our world: pollution, starvation of the young in our own country and of many in other parts of the world, the insensibilities of urban environments, these and others we speak of every day.

Technology suggests the mind and the use of rational processes. Not all that is rational is good, of course. But by and large, history points to the relief of much human misery through the use of the mind.

But this is not enough. To have effective rational processes available for the use of mankind does not insure that they will be used to relieve suffering. Too often they have been used to promote private greed and individual desire. More is indeed needed.

So it is that this school has affirmed throughout its history that man alone is insufficient. Man alone is not supreme. Man unaided cannot cope with his personal misery and with the agonies of his world.

In this place, therefore, and in our own rooms and together in other places, we ask the Almighty God for the strength to develop our own persons, our own talents, and through our petitionary acknowledgment that we alone are unequal to our tasks, we seek the fulfilling powers that lie within us, and we yearn for the wisdom and direction for our lives that they may not be led in vain.

As we mark our world's problems, we strain to find and develop our own capacities, searching then in the redeeming powers of humility and compassion and love for a life that will have meaning. In this sense it is not easy to be alive, if we are to be aware of the needs of our world and our capacity to help meet them. But living is also a matter of joy. If with Royster we cannot find a single theme for the rest of this school year, let us acknowledge a composite of themes: an Age of Joy, an Age of Wonder, an Age of Questioning, an Age of Hard Work. These and many other things this year will be.

We begin the life of this new school with confidence, with determination, and with happiness that we are all here, especially the girls; with knowledge of the many things to be done; with knowledge of the support and help we can find from each other, from teachers, and from students, if we ask for it; above all, with joyful anticipation for the work and the pleasures of the days ahead.

Let us pray.

Almighty God, we beseech thee with thy gracious favor to behold our universities, colleges, and schools, that knowledge may be increased among us, and all good learning flourish and abound. Bless all who teach and all who learn; and grant that in humility of heart they may ever look unto thee, who are the fountain of all wisdom; through Jesus Christ our Lord. Amen.

—*Chapel, January 6, 1971*

Shore Country
Day School Graduation

Bill's rapidly expanding duties as rector did not keep him from sharing his wisdom and experience with other educational institutions. In this speech at the closing exercises of the Shore Country Day School in Beverly, Massachusetts, on June 10, 1971, he explains—with great good humor and succinctness—his belief in the concepts of change and growth as the essence of the educational experience.

MR. BARTON, Mr. Whiting, Mr. Walsh, the Faculty, the Board of Trustees, parents and friends, students, and graduates of the day: As I begin, I would like to express my respect for Mr. Whiting and wish him well as he starts his retirement from the school.

It is a pleasure indeed for me to be here with you today, and I thank you for inviting me. Our schools, Shore and St. Paul's, have had a long association through students and faculties and parents. We share alumni and, I suppose, we often compete for their attention and support. Further, I believe there is a substantial congruency and overlap between the educational objectives of both schools, even though we operate at different age levels, an affinity of aspirations that characterizes our endeavors separately, which has assured a reasonably smooth voyage for those who move from one school to the other. For these, and for many other reasons, then, I have looked forward with pleasure to being here with you today.

As far as the next few minutes are concerned, however—that is, the commencement speech aspect of the day—I must confess other feelings. Addresses on such occasions are formidable. You hear so frequently that the formality of commencement ceremonies stifles speakers, though of course you also hear that they do not stifle them enough. At any rate, one must view the preparation and delivery of a commencement speech with some awe and with some doubts about one's ability to perform satisfactorily and to meet minimum expectations, particularly in length.

Happily for me, my tensions were greatly relieved several weeks ago, during our alumni weekend, our Anniversary, when, during the course of entertaining our twenty-fifth reunion class, I began asking a few questions about the commencement speaker they had had twenty-five years earlier. Of the thirty-seven men present, the number of those who could not remember the name of the speaker was thirty-seven. And no one had the vaguest idea of the topic to which the speaker had addressed himself.

I have to confess I was no help to the twenty-fifth class either, because, though I had attended their graduation, I also did not remember anything about their commencement speaker. The comforting conclusion of all this, then, is the fact that if we can get through this day and perhaps make it to Sunday and next week, nothing much will matter, as, mercifully, we will begin to forget whatever has happened here.

Probably you will be relieved to know that I shall ignore all issues of global significance in my remarks—issues such as the right of assembly and petition, the meaning of individual privacy in the age of the computer, the age of technological miniaturization, the meaning and proper application of force in a highly complex society, the needs of minorities, the population explosion, the changing role of women, the environment, hunger, civil rights, Vietnam. We need, and must, and do deal with these issues in our lives, but please relax. I shall not deal with any of these issues this particular morning.

I do want to speak for a few minutes on a very simple topic. The fact that it is simple does not mean that it is unimportant. And the simplicity of the topic does not mean that it will be easy for me to convey my thoughts to you, either. I shall speak about a simple matter that is of great importance, and the sophistication of the topic will require careful attention from you if you are going to be with me six minutes from now. I suppose what I am saying is, the time to begin listening carefully has arrived. Up to now you and I have been warming up. We have been getting acquainted. Now here we go in search of a shred of meaning that may redeem your patience and the morning.

Each student who graduates from this school today, in moving to another school and another community next year, has the unique opportunity of changing himself: of altering his habits and his life patterns and the public face he presents to others, so that in reputation, and in the thoughts of others, he can become quite a different person from what he has been before.

What happens to each of us, in the town where we are born, and in the school where we spend our first years, is that we become a definite person. Others come to have definite expectations of us. Then, we grow. We have experiences. We begin to see new life patterns for ourselves. But we also discover it is extremely difficult for us to move affirmatively to a new self, to a changed person, because our friends hold us firmly in their thoughts to what we have been.

The author Jerzy Kosinski calls this situation hell. "Hell," he writes, "is the inability to escape from others who prove and prove again to you that you are as they see you."

The uniqueness in graduation is that we leave those people behind. We move from one community to another, and thereby we gain the opportunity of starting all over, from the beginning.

Now why should we consider starting all over? Why should we even think of questioning our personalities, our life patterns, our attitudes, our habits, our selves? Haven't we done pretty well? We are big men and women on the Shore campus. We have excelled in plays and in writing, in athletics, in our many activities, in our class work. We have Shore firmly in our grasp. Things are pretty good, pretty comfortable. Why change?

I have already mentioned one reason to consider change, that arising from self-perception. In growing up, as we experience new situations, we find the urge to change welling up within us. Furthermore, our experiences in one institution, in comparison with the entire world out there, are somewhat parochial. We may have developed patterns of achievement and comfortable relationships with fellow students and faculty, so that all manner of glorious things can be said about us, and yet these relationships and triumphs are locally oriented and belong to one particular small community.

This is true no matter what the single institution is we talk about, whether it is Shore or St. Paul's. I understand there are some who believe that even Harvard is not the whole world, particularly when some of the Harvard theories and proposals, when tried, prove to be no more effective than other theories and proposals.

Let us consider a school illustration to establish this point for schools. Benjamin Bloom, writing in the Winter 1971 issue of the professional publication of the University of Chicago Graduate School of Education, refers to two schools, located in different states, that have vastly different student bodies. Both schools have taken a common set of achievement tests. Results show only minimal overlap. That is, the best students in one school have made test scores that rank them with the bottom students at the other school. In other words, in absolute terms, using test scores as the measure of performance, students ranking at the top in one school are equivalent in achievement to those students who stand at the bottom in the other school.

You can anticipate my next point, I am sure. Namely, that attitudes within the two schools are similar. Those achieving at the top receive praise and prizes, in both schools. And those at the bottom are congratulated for being there and for finishing out the year, but limited success is forecast for them.

Yet those at the bottom in one school, you will remember, have, the tests tell us, equivalent abilities to those at the top in the other. Such is the unreliability of local situations. Abundant confidence that stems from one social setting is suspect. Rigidity in attitude, based upon achievement, upon making it, in one community, is suspect.

Which leads us back to the entry point for this diversion: the justification for questioning one's life pattern when it is based upon experiences in the school, and in the community, in which one spends one's early years.

One of my college roommates acted on this principle for some months. He believed that meeting a person for the first time gave him an opportunity to try out a new personality. He carefully considered various kinds of roles for himself, from aggressive to meek, from studious and intellectual to carefree. And he lived each of these roles for a few hours. Following each such experiment he had a period of appraisal, to consider how effective he had been.

How much he learned is not really the point here. Rather I would suggest the willingness to experiment, to cast aside rigidities in one's personality, to test oneself under various pressures and conditions, above all, not to assume that whatever it is I am is what I must remain—these are the important aspects of this man's experimentations.

Jesus taught long ago: "Verily, verily, I say unto thee, Except a man be born again, he cannot see the kingdom of God" (John 3:3). The possibility of renewal, of regeneration, of starting anew, in the sense that I have been discussing it this morning, was, I am convinced, what Jesus had in mind in this sermon.

So I return to those who graduate, who today commence a new life. You will all go elsewhere next year. You are, I know, filled with excitement and curiosity and anticipation about new classes, new athletics, plays, school newspapers and literary magazines, debating societies, and the many other activities that will make up your school life next year. This is as it should be.

I suggest that you look at yourself, also. Your attitudes, your point of view, your personality, your habits. Now is the time to consider change for yourself. Now is the time in your life when you can have a fresh start if you want it.

Congratulations. Good luck to each of you. And thank you again for asking me to be with you today.

—*Shore Country Day School, June 10, 1971*

Discipline

Bill devoted the 1972 Annual Report of the Rector—his third—to the subject of discipline, and what was meant by the word at St. Paul's School. In the report he chose to define the term as "a relationship between people, usually with the connotation that one person is directing or leading or helping another person to act in a manner or way that person would not normally choose for himself." He was clearly giving the whole matter a great deal of thought in these days, and in this talk to the faculty before the start of the 1972 Winter Term, one can almost hear him developing and elaborating on those thoughts aloud, in what amounts to a kind of rough draft of what would become the annual report. One also absorbs a vivid sense of Bill's management style, his polite but firm insistence on pressing his considered agenda. This talk is really two talks in one: the first about discipline and the second about leadership. His point, of course, was that those qualities are in the end inextricably linked.

I PLAN TODAY to spend the rest of the session this morning in a discussion of discipline, and as much time as we want to this afternoon. There is no other business for the faculty today.

I have long felt it important to have a discussion that was not under time pressures. When discipline was last discussed in the faculty meeting, and in other considerations by the Dispatch of Business [committee] and the Heads [of Houses] since, it was suggested that the discussion begin with a statement by me of my personal point of view. This I shall now do. And in addition, I want to make certain proposals for the faculty to consider.

As a result of the faculty discussion this morning and this afternoon, there will be some decisions, I think. A decision to carry on as we have been doing, or decisions on modification of our present practice. But some kind of decision, some areas of decision and agreement among ourselves, both specific and implicit, are likely results of our discussions today, in my opinion. Agreements about all important school matters depend greatly upon members of the faculty—their understanding and their willingness and ability to carry them out.

We cannot expect, save in a few instances, to arrive at unanimous agreement among the faculty on complicated issues. Nevertheless, we can look carefully for consensus and majority attitudes. And at the same time we can be mindful of the qualitative voice of disagreement—even if that voice is a single person—as a restraint of some potency on the validity of the majority.

It is important for each of us today, then, to participate appropriately and carefully, because we are fashioning for ourselves a position from which we shall be working individually. And in our work we shall be depending upon the cooperation and work of others, as we all move in the same direction. It will be important for us, particularly this afternoon, as we move along, to have some understanding of what it is we seem to be saying, and what it is we seem to be agreeing upon.

I shall try as best as I can to keep this before us in summary form, so we shall know what it is we are talking about and what it is we are saying and apparently agreeing to. But I shall also appreciate your help with this. Presiding and summarizing are not particularly easy things to do simultaneously. Please help us as a group with this.

Our meeting this morning and this afternoon, then, will be in two parts: First, a statement by me of my general point of view on discipline. Second, thereafter, a general discussion by the faculty pointed toward consideration of some of our practices, modifications of these practices, and agreements about procedures.

Let us recognize frankly what I am about to do. I am going to discuss discipline and its relation to our general activities from my own point of view. It is not news to anyone in this room that I do not have an international reputation as a supreme authority on the subject of discipline. I am under no illusions that my opinions and attitudes are "right" in the sense that "true facts" are "true." But anyone who has worked in education, anyone who has spent some or many years in activities with the young—and this includes parents—will have, and should have, some definite points of view on the subject. I do. And I think it is useful for us at this time for me to discuss these viewpoints, both as an expression of the opinions and attitudes of the headmaster of this school, and as an individual response (which many people in this room are well qualified to make) to give us a starting point for our faculty discussion.

What is discipline? Where would we go, and what would we look for, if we want to see or feel or sense discipline? What does the word mean? What concept does this shorthand word evoke that stands for a phrase that stands for infinities of meanings? In other words, what is it we are talking about?

I would like to suggest that discipline is leadership. Discipline as a word has a rather harsh ring to it. Some years ago we shifted terminology in this school, attempting to substitute the word "activities" for discipline. Our committee on discipline disappeared, and another committee took over its place and responsibilities. The idea behind this shift was sound and useful, I think. As a word, discipline has a negative connotation, whereas the general area of concerns is both affirmative and negative.

In one sense I would suggest that the concepts behind our use of the word "discipline" are those of leadership. Or, perhaps a better word, facilitation, in the sense that our purpose is to promote the effectiveness of a course of conduct, the effectiveness of the educational activities of this school. But I think we would have to respond that it is an element of the educational process or, in more general terms, an element present in all social units, organized and unorganized, implicit and explicit.

There is a certain element of discipline involved, I think, when in a one-to-one situation, walking on the street toward a person who is approaching me, we agree

74

silently yet effectively not to collide. That one of us will go in one direction, the other in the other direction. Here there is unspoken communication which results in a mutually satisfactory conclusion that allows both people to continue on their way.

The reverse situation I observed in New York City on December 15, while taxis were attempting to enter the Queens Midtown Tunnel, as I was on my way to LaGuardia to return to Concord following the hockey game. A large bus and a taxi both attempted, mindlessly, to inch into the same bit of land space in this more or less Oklahoma land-rush scene, which was not showing off the citizens of New York City at their best anyway. And the result was, each hopped from his seat, and the two men began banging away at each other, this following a heated verbal exchange of opinions and insults. Actual fighting on the streets of Fun City. Incidentally, the taxi driver got the best of it. I don't know what this proves about big-city virility, but that is the fact.

My point is that discipline as a concept refers to relationships in a social unit of some kind. For us, the unit is this educational institution. Discipline is one element of our life together.

Hence the conclusion that I am reaching for is that discipline must be considered by us in the context of the institution, and within the total context of the purposes of this school. Discipline is an essential property of any educational institution and may be discussed as a separate force—but the discussion must be rooted in general direction of the institution itself. As a general thing, then, let us consider discipline in the wider concepts of leadership and facilitation.

At this point I think we have to give some consideration to our understanding of the fundamental properties of this school. What is its primary purpose? To give a brief answer, and without spending a great deal of time on this important question, because that is not the principal purpose of our discussion today, I would say: to assist the young students in this school in the development of their talents and abilities. John Dewey, long ago, wrote that "education is precisely the work of supplying the conditions which will enable the psychic functions, as they successively arise, to mature and pass into higher functions in the freest and fullest manner."

We are working in Piaget's fourth stage, that of logical and cognitive development. Piaget's fourth stage is the final stage, from age eleven to adulthood, the era of development of formal-operational thought. I want to read a brief description of this fourth stage in Piaget's formulation.

In the era of eleven to adulthood, in the development of formal-operational thought, the following are the principal things that take place:

Inferences through logical operations upon propositions, or "operations upon operations."

Reasoning about reasoning.

Construction of systems of all possible relations or implications.

Hypothetico-deductive isolation of variables and testing of hypotheses.

True formal thought.
Construction of all possible combinations of relations, systematic isolation of variables, and deductive hypothesis-testing.

These are the major generalities we are engaged in teaching. Or, we are present when these capacities emerge and develop in our young students. This says nothing, of course, about more familiar objectives that we talk about all the time: gaining admission to Yale or some other specific college, or acquiring specific knowledge and facilities in subject matter areas such as geometry and literature and history, and the others.

And, lest we think it is "easy" for the adolescent to develop these elements of formal-operational thought, as defined by Piaget, let me suggest that tentative results from careful testing indicate that perhaps as many as one-half of American citizens do not develop these capacities, ever—that they spend their adult lives in a preadolescent stage of mental development.

There is much for us to do, to help ensure that as many as possible (perhaps all) of our students begin to achieve, or do achieve, these capacities for formal-operational thought as well as the achievement of certain levels of specific knowledge, to which we are correctly devoted. What I am saying is that, in my opinion, our primary focus is, and should be, upon the development of our students; that our task as a school, again to use Dewey's words, is "the work of supplying the conditions which will enable the psychical functions, as they successively arise, to mature and pass into higher functions, in the freest and fullest manner."

To use shorthand concepts, our primary task is not to assure that every student in school can score a 700, or any specific number, on one or all of his College Board examinations. Rather, as I said a moment ago, it is to assist our young students in the development of their talents and abilities. As teachers, in the classroom, I suspect we all face two general methods of operation. We can conduct a class with detailed direction and support, hoping thereby to achieve the maximum performance on the specifics of our subject matter from each student. Or, so to speak, we can hang back. We can open doors, look out on vistas, remove major roadblocks, but make no attempt to lead everyone to the furthest possible point for him as an individual. We thus leave to the initiative and interest of the individual student the determination of how far he will go at that particular moment.

Probably it is safe to say that with our younger students, and for the most part with introductory materials, first-year languages, early mathematics, grammar, and so on, we adopt the first method. With older students, with more sophisticated materials, the second approach is more generally adopted and is generally more appropriate and more effective. It is my opinion that neither method is appropriate for all situations. And further, that the second method must be ours in most, if not all, of our work at least by the fifth form, perhaps the fourth form.

Similarly, in discipline I would suggest there are two polar positions. First, shall we say on the right, the position of detailed instruction and rules. Everything, every aspect of behavior, is specified. As an extreme, perhaps prisons and the military are examples here. Secondly, at the other end—perhaps at the left—is the position of laissez-faire. Anything goes. The individual is the judge of the details of his conduct. I am not quite sure what to cite as examples of this position. Perhaps the fantasies of the young, or some of the young. Timothy Leary's response to the refusal of Switzerland to extradite him to the United States: he called this a great act of love. Probably it was a carefully calculated political decision taken at the highest level of the Swiss government.

At any rate, there is a compelling attraction for many of us in the thought that we can develop statements and regulations and exhortations that will indicate clearly, once and for all, what kind of behavior is acceptable. But this appearance is, I think, illusory, not only because in practical terms it really cannot be done. The military have their courts martial. Penology has its Atticas. Society had slave riots in Roman times. But more important, this approach to behavior or leadership or discipline contradicts the fundamental principles of our broad educational responsibilities and opportunities, as I have discussed these this morning.

Detailed prescription leaves no room for development. It provides only for achievement. This is not satisfactory, in my opinion. One point of interpretation here has great importance for us, I think. A study carried out three or four years ago sought to measure and differentiate the perceptions of children concerning the affection and love held by their parents for them, based upon the attitudes held by parents toward child rearing. Parents were divided into seven categories, extending, again from the left, from parents who had an extreme "permissive" attitude toward their children, to the far right, to parents who believed they should control the behavior of their children in an extreme authoritarian way. The interesting result was that the children of parents in both extreme groups had similar attitudes or perceptions about the love and concern their parents held for them. Both groups of children felt the least love and concern from their parents.

One way of interpreting this is to say that the authoritarian parents were devoted to achieving precise behavior, regardless of any other objective, and hence love played little part in their thoughts. And similarly, permissive parents were resigning interest and concern in their children with a blanket vote of approval for conduct of any kind whatsoever.

To sum up a bit: I think our responsibility is to seek to supply and support the conditions in which personal development can take place. I think our primary focus and hope and objective is that as much personal development as possible will take place. With discipline this means, I think, that we are recognizing the fact that we shall not always have acceptable behavior. We can discuss at length—and this is precisely the purpose of our meetings today—the location of boundaries.

If we are too rigid, we run the risk of stunting growth and development. If our boundaries and limits are too broad or too dimly perceived, we run the risk of conditions that similarly will block personal development. I would suggest that, though we might like to have a school in which everyone behaves perfectly according to our own collective standards, we do not have this as an objective to be achieved.

Rather, I think we must have our expectations at important points stated in ways that present choices for students so that in their responses, and particularly in owning their responses and the consequences that flow from choices, their own personal development can take place.

One final broad, general point, and then I shall come to some specifics. Let us not overlook the vast complexities of the lives of adolescents, simply because these complexities have been so often stated and because we, having reached adulthood, have pulled ourselves through the other side into a unified and committed maturity.

Individually, the tensions and complexities of the years twelve to eighteen are staggering and overwhelming. In dealing with our school, with our total student population, we must remember not only individual responses to adolescence but also the immense amount of variability that is not age-related.

The sequence of biological changes in adolescence is unchanged, probably for at least five thousand years: girls still develop two years earlier than boys; some boys have completed their whole bodily adolescent development before other boys of the same chronological age have begun theirs. The start of the process of physical change in adolescence occurs at a far earlier time now than in earlier generations, two years earlier in American society than was true just forty years ago.

It is important for us to remember the enormous variability among boys at ages thirteen, fourteen, and fifteen, who will range all the way from practically complete maturity to absolute preadolescence. The similar age range for girls is eleven, twelve, and thirteen. This means that most girls will have begun physical adolescent change before entering school, and many will be approaching maturity, whereas many third- and fourth-form boys will not have begun the adolescent spurt or will be encountering only its initial stages.

What this suggests is that our student body of 480 students is composed of boys and girls who are at widely different stages in adolescence. That these differences are not age-related and therefore are not confined to certain sections only of the school. That we do have wide variability in maturity in all forms and in all class and other student groups. This is further evidence, for me, of the necessity for our concentration upon personal development as opposed to absolutist expectations—absolutes of achievement, absolutes in expectations of behavior.

I now come to specifics. I am first going to discuss my own understanding of discipline, or leadership, in one-to-one or small group relationships. After completing this, I shall come to some specific comments about discipline presently in school and some proposals for us as a faculty to consider. I hope this will be helpful.

These comments are primarily personal observation and belief, based upon my own experiences, my own experimentation, my own analysis of my personal actions and results achieved. I am discussing my personal experiences and the beliefs that flow from these experiences because this has been suggested to me as perhaps a useful thing to do. At any rate, it amounts to one case history. There is no suggestion of broad, refined intellectual analysis. There is no implication that these are the "best" or "correct" responses and comments. These are simply my own experiences and attitudes, in all their nakedness.

The Boy Scout movement was in full flower in Aberdeen, South Dakota, when I turned twelve. I joined. At age thirteen years and six months I became an Eagle Scout, a rather early age to accomplish the necessary requirements. I will refrain from interpreting myself, at this or any other time, in terms of concentration upon achievement rather than development!

At any rate, at age thirteen years and nine months I found myself a tent leader for ten weeks at Boy Scout summer camp, and I spent the two following summers in increasingly more responsible leadership positions in the Boy Scout summer camps.

While an undergraduate in college, and for two summers while working on my master's degree in history, I was a counselor at Mowglis, a camp for boys on Newfound Lake sixty miles north of Concord, under a remarkable camp director, Colonel Elwell, who influenced generations of boys over a period of forty years and whose influence on me and them continues.

For one year at Shady Side Academy in Pittsburgh, and ten years in this school, I was a full-time teacher, coach, and dormitory housemaster. As you know, I have three sons and, happily for me, no direct responsibility for two daughters-in-law, except the pleasures that come to all of us in their having joined our family.

I have had no military leadership experience, and in fact only the briefest exposure to the military in Germany and England at the end of the war in an analytical-historical group called the United States Strategic Bombing Survey, where I did writing, editing, and translations.

It is on the basis of these sets of experiences that I speak of my own personal point of view toward leadership, or discipline.

First, there needs to be clarity: of views, of desires, of expectations. This does not mean that everything must have the clarity of "Don't touch" for the child-and-hot-stove situation. But clarity of what the tolerances are, what the boundaries are, and where they are located.

Second, consistency. The force of leadership dissolves in the presence of inconsistency. Contradictory signals lead nowhere.

Third, compassion. Heart. Humanity. Both the variety of "mistakes are sometimes made," and the variety that the leader is the last to bed at night, retiring only after everyone is safe, secure, and happy, and the first up in the morning to test the conditions of the day, to check out the plausibility of yesterday's plans for today, to make preparations. Leadership requires constant thoughtfulness for others. The self comes last if at all. Or at some other time like vacations.

Fourth, fairness. No grudges. A leader vitiates his effectiveness with responses based on personalities, in addition to being unfair. There is no room for grudges.

Fifth, candor. Honesty to oneself and to others. There is no room for displaced aggression.

Sixth, coolness. Do not react or respond in anger or in elation. There are places to express anger and elation and other personal emotions, which support leadership in demonstrating its humanity. But knee-jerk responses based on anger or elation, or other emotions, can confuse and vitiate effectiveness.

Seventh, thoroughness. Follow-through. Detail-mindedness. A leader must be prepared to subordinate everything when it is necessary to concentrate and act upon a single aspect of his responsibility. Particularly, to make clear a point with a person for whom he has some responsibility, he must be ready to throw himself into a situation, forgetting all else, until the point is made. And later, in extra time that comes out of his own hide, he must attend appropriately to all other responsibilities neglected in the interim.

Eighth, the big picture. The general setting can never be lost sight of. The leader must constantly be looking down the road, perceiving what is coming a day or a year later, determining what things need to be done this morning or this week, in order to set the stage for the successful further development of whatever it is he is responsible for.

This is the end of this set of specifics. I hope I have not bored you—too much.

These are the principal elements, explained briefly, presented not necessarily in order of importance, which for me have comprised the essence of leadership over the years. You will recognize that I have spoken in terms of individual or small-group leadership. When these elements are considered in terms of a large social setting, this school, with many actual leaders, that is, the members of the faculty, different interpretations and emphases result. I am not going to attempt this interpretation. I only point out that differences exist.

Finally, specifics about St. Paul's School, and the present moment of time in our history. I believe we became careless last term at places where we should not be careless. I think we should make a rather substantial change this term, starting today at this moment. We should insist upon full meeting of school responsibilities in attendance at classes, seated meals, and chapel. We should discuss whether breakfast should be added to this list. Certainly all athletic commitments, all commitments for participation in extracurricular activities, responsibilities in houses for decent performance—these matters should be included.

I think we as faculty must meet fully our own personal responsibilities so that we can know what students are doing. We must meet every class. We should attend all chapel services. We should keep absence from seated meals to an absolutely irreducible minimum; perhaps the best minimum should be zero, at least for the Winter Term, perhaps for the rest of this year.

I think all absences must be reported: students must be expected to sit at assigned seats for seated meals, and if they are missing, they must be reported, and the system of reporting must be carried on thoroughly and accurately.

Absence from class, from athletic commitments or elsewhere, should be reported to Mr. Hill's office. We need to be aware of any absence from chapel, and this must be reported. This can be done either informally if every member of the faculty is present in chapel and is observant of absences, and turns notification in to Mr. Hill's office. Or it can be done formally through the assignment of certain sections of chapel rows to each member of the faculty.

Finally, there must be thorough follow-through for every reported absence, and some school response. I would suggest that the demerit system for forms one through four continue as presently constituted, and that this system not be extended to the fifth and sixth forms. I would suggest, however, that any absence from class, chapel, or seated meals (with a decision by the faculty on breakfast) be responded to by placing the student "on restriction" for two weeks.

The result, if all of these recommendations I have made are the consensus of this faculty, and particularly, then, if these understandings are acted upon with consistency and compassion, with fairness, candor, clarity, coolness, and thoroughness, the result will be a rather substantial change in the school. At first hearing you may conclude that my recommendations are inconsistent with my general discussion of the objectives of discipline, or leadership, as these are rooted in my understanding of the purpose of this school.

I myself do not find inconsistency. Rather I think we are faced with matters of emphasis. We moved in the fall too far, perhaps unknowingly, in the direction of laissez-faire. We need, I think, to move to the right in the direction of more specific indicators of expected behavior, accompanied by actions that convey the full meaning of these indicators.

We should not confuse the variability which we have introduced into the school, the variety of course offerings, the changes in diploma requirements, the extension of work in areas of performance and experience, the arts and independent study, the greater sensitivity to individual needs, and conclude that we are operating without structure. Indeed, basic structure as a reference point is vitally necessary to the successful accomplishment of the variability of student activities. We want these variations. We earnestly desire and need these new experiences, and these old experiences clad in new forms. But at the same time we need basic structure. Perhaps we have confused, this fall, these two matters. We are extending and developing variability, but this does not mean that anything goes. We must stand firm with certain points of basic structure.

My suggestion, then, is to deepen and make more clear the basic structure. As and when this flourishes, variability can float with purpose and meaning overhead. Or at least around, perhaps below. We need now, and later today, to move into consideration of any of these matters, to consideration of these recommendations, to receiving other recommendations if anyone wishes to make them, and to considering whatever is presented.

—*Winter 1972*

Sportsmanship

Bill may have been wholly immersed in cajoling the school into the late twentieth century, but in other ways he was a man of almost Victorian rectitude. In this chapel talk on good sportsmanship on January 31, 1972, he exhorts his listeners to truly learn those things on earth, the knowledge of which continues into the heavens. And, of course, to "never forget to be kind." Four years later, at the start of the spring term, he delivered a brief order, a mandamus that reflected his commitment to a worthy amenity which appeared to be in eclipse—over his dead body!

YOU WILL RECALL, I am sure, my speaking to the school last term on the subject of sportsmanship, the responsibilities of the spectator at athletic games, and in particular spectator sportsmanship as we watch hockey games in the Gordon Rink. The conduct of some of us, in my judgment, had been completely unsatisfactory. That miserable chant: "You, you, you," with fingers pointed in unison at an opponent. Cheers carrying the message of a derisive boo when an opponent had some bit of bad luck.

I asked you to stop this kind of conduct. Or more correctly, I asked that you consider the positive, affirmative responsibilities of a spectator at a game so that good play could be supported, and so there could be genuine happiness and joy with St. Paul's victories.

Thank you for your cooperation. More important, I would commend you for the thinking I am sure you have engaged in, and for your decision, as a result of your own consideration, that positive and affirmative responses are the correct responses—the only responses—for a spectator.

Recently I had a very unhappy afternoon. I drove to another school, a well-known school, a so-called "good" school you know—one that is good like us—to watch our hockey team play. Early in the first period one of our players got a penalty as a result of eager, hard play. There was no indication of maliciousness or meanness, but as our player skated to the penalty box the chant of "You, you, you" rocketed through the rink, spectators vigorously exercising their fingers as they pointed and their lungs as they shouted. And in the minutes that followed, this negative spectator participation picked up steam, as is always true in such a situation of group enthusiasm, positive or negative. With three minutes to go in the first period, one of our players was checked hard near the boards, resulting in a penalty for the opponent—something that is part of the game and entirely to be expected. But, as our player was attempting to extricate himself from the tangle of arms and legs of which he was a part, a student spectator reached over the boards and hit our player on the head. Not a friendly tap. Not a gesture of helpfulness as our player tried to get back on his feet. No, it was a hard bang on the head.

Now don't worry about our players. The point of this story is not to enlist your sympathy for our player. He responded as he had every right to do, with three or four heavy blows on the student spectator who had not quite expected that reaction, and indeed was not ready for it. The student spectator was quite happy, I thought, to have the referee stop the whole business. The referee warned the school headmaster, who then came on the public address system to ask spectators not to interfere with the game, but, while he was speaking, a series of hisses came from the students.

The game continued two more periods with negative spectator conduct chants of "You, you, you," and jeers and cheers at the wrong time. The atmosphere in the rink was brittle. It was unpleasant. And it made the playing of the game an unhappy occasion, not the pleasant combat it should have been.

I tell you this unhappy story this morning, not to criticize the students in another school who are unable to explain themselves. No, I tell you this because this experience has made me all the more ashamed of this school last fall—ashamed of our conduct at any time when we are in the least guilty of miserable sportsmanship.

I ask again today, as I did last fall: Who wants to win through the use of unfair tactics? Who cares about victory if it comes through unfair methods? Let us think of our own responsibilities. Let us strive for good sportsmanship and hard play and victories. Let us applaud and cheer good play, no matter who performs it, an opponent or our own player. Let us give others a fair chance to beat us, while working with all our power to play to the utmost of our abilities to triumph.

Hemingway wrote once that courage is grace under pressure. Pressures there will always be in our lives. Let us look for, let us pray for, the divine grace that will let us act courageously. Let us win, but first and foremost, let us live fairly.

Would you turn to page 24 in the *Chapel Services and Prayers* book. Let us join in saying the prayer at the top of this page. Let us pray.

Grant, O Lord, that in all the joys of life we may never forget to be kind. Help us to be unselfish in friendship, thoughtful of those less happy than ourselves, and eager to bear the burdens of others; through Jesus Christ our Savior. Amen.

—January 31, 1972

Shaking Hands

I T IS A SCHOOL CUSTOM, as we all know, that returning students at the start of a term shake hands with the
rector. Many of you accomplished this yesterday between
5:30 and 6:30 in the Schoolhouse, but some of you did not
come there.

When chapel is over, will those of you who did not
come to the Schoolhouse last evening pursue me to the
altar end of the chapel, where I shall be to complete this
pleasant ritual.

—*April 1, 1976*

William A. Oates, the eighth rector of St. Paul's School, from 1970 to 1982, reads "reports" after chapel, spring 1972.

Bill with his first wife, the former Margaret Nichols, after his arrival at St. Paul's. (Margie Oates died in 1965.)

The Oates family at home in the 1950s: Bill Sr. and Margie with sons Billy (William Jr.), Thomas (in shorts), and James.

Two decades later, in the 1970s, two generations of Oates men:
Bill Sr. (standing rear), Billy (left), Jim (center), and Tom (right).

Board of Trustees and new rector in 1970. Front row, left to right:
Amo Houghton, president; Tom Rodd; Bill Oates, rector; Bishop
Hall; Percy Chubb. Second row: John McLane; August Heckscher;
Sam Calloway; Bill Moore; Rowlie Stebbins. Top row: Oz Elliott;
John Q. Adams; Walker Lewis; Kaighn Smith; Benjy Neilson.

In 1975 the rector congratulates Ralph T. Starr, '44, chairman of the
Fund for SPS, and Fund director and vice rector Robert E. Duke.

Bill shares a light moment on the chapel steps with administrative assistant Coolidge M. 'Cal' Chapin '35.

In 1973 the rector announces "Cricket Holiday," a surprise day-off and a cherished ritual.

Under Bill's leadership, diversity quietly became a reality. In 1975 he presents Rector's Awards to Randa E. Wilkinson and Claude E. Sloan Jr.

*Art Department master William Abbe's graphic pastiche celebrates
Bill's sixtieth birthday—and 34th year at St. Paul's—in 1976.*

With his wife, Jean, in 1981 Bill celebrates St. Paul's School's 125th anniversary—a year before he retires after four decades at SPS.

The Oates Performing Arts Center made manifest Bill's belief that the arts are central elements of education and life.

Overleaf: The rector addresses students, faculty, families, and friends gathered for graduation in 1981.

A decade after retiring from St. Paul's, Bill accepts an award for service to Harvard from fellow alumnus Albert Gordon.

Part Three

AT·FULL·TILT

Tolerance

As Bill moved toward the midpoint of his rectorship—the dramatic transition to coeducation behind him and the modernization of the school now well under way—he felt even freer to articulate his educational philosophy and vision for St. Paul's. He reflected often on the importance of tolerance—and ambiguity—in a school setting. He grappled, slowly and calmly, with the last piece of the coeducation puzzle: how and when to allow boys and girls to visit each other in their dorms. He also placed new and emphatic importance on the place of the arts in the formal curriculum. Invariably, he approached all such questions from the perspective of his deep immersion in educational and development theory, concepts he had first studied at Harvard but never stopped exploring.

At the start of the first post-Watergate presidential election year, Bill delivered a chapel talk that emphasized the quest for the eternal verities that still obtain, even in an era of new openness and discord for the nation and the school. This talk is revealing in its vivid reflection of the careful line Bill always walked between reverence for the cherished traditions of the school and society, and acceptance of the diversity of views that make for healthy give and take in both settings.

THE MORNING LESSON is found in the thirteenth chapter of the Gospel According to Matthew, beginning at the twenty-fourth verse:

> Jesus put before them another parable, saying: "The kingdom of heaven may be compared to a man who sowed good seed in his field; but while men were sleeping, his enemy came and sowed weeds among his wheat, and went away. So when the plants came up and bore grain, then the weeds appeared also. And the servants of the householder came and said to him: 'Sir, did you not sow good seed in your field? How then has it weeds?' And he said to them, 'An enemy has done this.' The servants said to him, 'Then do you want us to go and gather them?' But he said, 'No; lest in gathering the weeds you root up the wheat along with them. Let both grow together until the harvest; and at harvest time I will tell the reapers, Gather the weeds first and bind them in bundles to be burned, but gather the wheat into my barn.'"

Here endeth the Morning Lesson.

Tolerance is one of man's noble virtues. Tolerance: the capacity to respect the beliefs and behavior of others. Tolerance of divergent views and actions is much needed in our world today.

The world of mechanics provides another explanation for the concept of tolerance, in this case meaning leeway for variation from a standard. The roof structure of a house may call for a beam, a piece of wood two by six and fourteen feet long. But the beam could be a fraction longer, or a fraction shorter, and still serve its purpose satisfactorily. In terms of engineering, the concept of tolerance provides for a permissible deviation from a specified value, and neither efficiency nor effectiveness is sacrificed.

In the parable, the growth of weeds in a field of wheat is tolerated or allowed. Have patience, declares the householder to his workers, who are ready to rush into the fields to pull up weeds helter-skelter. In time, at fruition, we shall take care of the situation adequately. We will gather the wheat and keep it, and we will discard the weeds. Right now we can accept what is going on in the field. For the present, we can tolerate the growth of both wheat and weeds.

Let us speculate for a moment about the reasons that probably lie behind this point of view. Why does the householder keep his workers away from the fields and not allow them to pull out the weeds? One reason, I suspect, is the difficulty of knowing for sure which plants are weeds, which plants are wheat.

Each spring I have a small garden just behind the rectory. I always plant lettuce seed. In the early weeks of growth, the lettuce plants are small, tender, and difficult to distinguish from the various kinds of weeds that grow without any encouragement from me. I find that I must be careful, deliberate, and slow as I work in the garden. I must be sure to identify a weed as a weed before pulling it up, or I will destroy my hope of having lettuce to eat later in the spring.

It was this way in the Old World as well. Darnel, as some of the wild grasses and weeds native to the Mediterranean areas were called, is almost indistinguishable from wheat until the time of harvest. The householder could not be sure that the weeds would in fact be pulled, and the wheat saved, if he allowed his workers to enter the fields.

We are frequently confronted with the same type of situation in looking at the actions of other people, and we wonder what they are doing and why. For example, at the circus the high-wire walker may quiver and almost fall. And the crowd will gasp and worry. But did the high-wire walker quiver because of his lack of skill? Or was there a sudden unexpected wind? Or was it all part of his act? In other words, was the quiver a purposive behavior, carried on in strict adherence to rules, for a reason: to entertain? Watching the high-wire act a second or a third time will produce support for one or the other of these interpretations, but the conclusion one reaches will still be a bit tentative and lack certainty.

So, too, in judging complicated situations in the lives of other people, or in our everyday school life, this difficulty is present. Is my view of a certain matter correct? Is my friend's view wrong? One reason for the need for tolerance is lack of certainty. In the absence of positive, universally accepted truth, a prudent person will be a bit tentative in his judgments. He will be tolerant. A prudent person cannot tell the darnel from the genuine wheat in the early stages of growth, so he is patient and waits for further evidence to appear at maturity.

Let us return now to general speculation about the reasons for the householder's decision in not allowing his workers to pull up the weeds before harvest time, even assuming they could tell the weeds from the grain successfully. We recall that he said, Do not go out to the fields to pull out the weeds "lest in gathering the weeds you root up the wheat along with them." While plants are still growing and developing, the experienced farmer takes care not to move the earth near the roots of his plants. For growth can be impeded, or even stopped, if the root system of a plant is greatly disturbed.

Looking now for a moment at our national life, we recognize that the country is in a very difficult position. The soil of national life is greatly disturbed as each week brings new information about human and political and official misconduct, assassination plots, illegal experimentation on human beings, and similar disheartening activities. Leaders of our American democratic government have acted in un-American, nondemocratic ways. The country is reeling from unending disclosures. As Russell Baker puts it, we are being ravaged by honesty. It is clear to all of us that the ultimate responsibility, the ultimate blame, so to speak, belongs with false leaders and their unconstitutional and immoral actions.

When there is evil in our national life, it must be revealed. I am not criticizing the investigative reporters. I am not proposing that we, like the emperor of Persia in earlier years, should behead the reporters of the *Washington Post* or the *New York Times*. That is not the point.

The point is that when the soil of national life becomes as disturbed as it is now, it is difficult for healthy, positive activities to take root and to grow. The capacity of our nation to support and encourage healthful and beneficial activities is seriously limited. I think that, as a nation, we must recognize this situation and work to restore stability to national life so that our roots may again become firm and growth may be encouraged and supported for healthful activities.

To summarize now, briefly, what I have been saying: tolerance does suggest that we act tentatively, that we recognize we cannot be positive at all times. Tolerance suggests that we act within the context of the totality of life. Will the final result of our action amount to an improvement in the entire situation?

A final characteristic of tolerance needs now to be mentioned. To some people, tolerance seems to imply acceptance of the views of others. It seems to say that all views are equally valuable. Well, not necessarily. As I have indicated this morning, there are other reasons for silence, for not attempting to smash the views or actions of others.

A person may feel a bit tentative about his own position. Or he may feel it will not be generally helpful to straighten out this one small bit of reality if, in so doing, damage is done in broader, larger, and more important respects. In fact the concept of tolerance implies a difference of views. I hold one view. Others hold other views. I am tolerant of those other views.

In other words, there would be no need for the concept of tolerance in human affairs if everyone agreed on everything. Tolerance implies differences. To tolerate is to respect the rights or opinions or practices of others, whether I agree with them or not—it is to allow without prohibition or opposition, without necessarily being in agreement.

Among different viewpoints, one is correct. Other views are wrong. As long as there is a purpose in the world, as long as there is a God, there is a right way and a wrong way. This we acknowledge.

Until the day of maturity, the harvest time, let the grasses grow. But then the wheat can be saved and the weeds discarded.

Woodrow Wilson wrote long ago of a "spirit of learning" as the way of freedom and reason, of mutual trust, civility, and respect for one another. It is only through such a generous spirit of learning, through free and open inquiry, that men can progress toward understanding.

Our country. Our society. Our school. In each there is a need for a "spirit of learning," for the spirit of tolerance. We need mutual trust, civility, and respect for one another.

But we also need conviction and belief. We must acknowledge there is a correct way, and we must seek it.

Let all views flourish as we seek truth in a constant and unwavering quest. May the spirit of learning be present in this school. May tolerance grow and flourish among us. May we maintain tentativeness of judgment and hold consideration for the full needs of others. At the same time, let us strive to deepen our own personal convictions, as we seek that which is right, and discard that which is wrong.

Let us pray.

—Chapel, January 11, 1976

On Teachers and Teaching

*Bill's chapel talks as rector invariably displayed his wide curiosity,
catholicity of interests, and general erudition on matters of pedagogy.
In this example from the first Sunday of the Spring Term of 1976—
a talk I remember vividly from my own student days—he uses the
examples of a world-famous artist and a beloved St. Paul's master to
underline the essential and undying role that good teaching plays in
the life of any school. In the process, he relates his post to the assigned
Bible lesson for the day—a reading from Solomon—in a way that
any clergyman might envy.*

THE MORNING LESSON is found in the seventh
chapter of the Wisdom of Solomon:

> Therefore I prayed, and prudence was given to me;
> I called for help, and there came to me a spirit of wis-
> dom. I valued her above sceptre and throne, and reck-
> oned riches as nothing beside her. . . . All was mine to
> enjoy, for all follows where wisdom leads, and I was in
> ignorance before. . . . What I learned with pure inten-
> tion I now share without grudging. . . .

God grant that I may speak according to his will, and that my own thoughts may be worthy of his gifts; for even wisdom is under God's direction, and he corrects the wise; we and our words, prudence, and knowledge and craftsmanship, all are in his hand.

Here endeth the Morning Lesson.

Ten days ago the *New York Times* reported on the life and influence of the artist Josef Albers, aged eighty-eight, who had just died. Albers was renowned throughout the world as a teacher of art and as the leading modern theorist of color. His books and his works reveal the infinite gradations, harmonies, and contrasts of color that are to be attained in patient experimentation and work. To preserve and focus the viewer's attention to his treatment of color, Albers restricted himself to the use of the square. Squares within squares, boxes within boxes—a simple geometric format which forced colors to yield their essences, one to another.

But it is Albers as teacher that I want to remember this morning. First at the Bauhaus in Weimar, his native Germany. Then, after 1933, at Black Mountain College in North Carolina. Finally at Yale, where he completed his teaching and artistic career. Over the course of his teaching years, Albers influenced generation after generation of artists with his theories and beliefs.

In 1969 a group of grateful students compiled a film in Albers' honor, testifying to his influence in their lives. One of the students [Robert Rauschenberg] had this to say in the film: "Albers was a beautiful teacher but an impossible person. His criticism was so devastating that

I wouldn't ask for it. But, twenty-one years later, I am still learning what he taught me."

I am learning, still, after twenty-one years, what he taught me. The present tense, to denote continued change and development; the past tense, to refer to what was taught but which nevertheless remains a living force to be accommodated, bit by bit. All that was taught can be learned only through an ongoing quest, a search that will not end. This is the influence of teachers.

I spent a day during spring vacation in Dallas with an alumnus of St. Paul's School, a 1923 graduate. Part of the afternoon we sat in my host's favorite room in his home, a room where glass cases filled with beautiful porcelain birds lined the walls. Birds lifelike in size and color—not an easy accomplishment when one remembers the uncertainties of final result when color pigment is fired.

Then we inspected my host's library, some four thousand books, every one a book about birds, said to be the most comprehensive and finest collection of books about birds in the world. Here was the first book on birds ever published, in 1557; giant folio volumes with full-color illustrations—color having been added by hand in the London print shops of the late eighteenth and nineteenth centuries, long before the advent of modern four-color printing processes. The birds of Asia, of South America, of Australia, of Europe, of America—in shelves from floor to ceiling.

"How did you acquire your interest in birds?" I finally asked, a modest understatement of a question.

"Well," my host responded, "St. Paul's School plays a very important role in this interest that has dominated my life. At the end of the Winter Term of my first year at school I became pretty sick, but I didn't want to tell anyone about it for fear that I would not be allowed to go home. By the time I arrived in New York to meet my mother, my appendix had ruptured, which required immediate surgery and a lot of worry for my mother. I came through it and returned to school, one week late for the start of the Spring Term, with instructions that I could not do any athletics. That was when I met Beach White."

Generations of St. Paul's students learned English from Beach White. He was on the faculty from 1896 until 1942, for many years serving as head of the English Department. Students learned about punctuation and sentence structure; about writing. They acquired a love of words from this remarkable man. Beach White was a formidable and persuasive teacher.

But there was something else about Beach White, beyond his influence in the classroom. Many students, my host in Dallas included, gained a lasting love of nature, and of birds in particular, through their association with him. Students learned many things when they walked with Beach White on the trails and hills that surround the school. A love of nature and animals and birds carried through their lives.

"I am still learning what he taught me." This is the influence of teachers.

Why, you may be wondering, should I talk this morning about artists and teachers? Because I have no doubt at all that in future years you will look back on your experiences here, and in particular to the devotion, attention, and care of your teachers, and you will be grateful. You will remember a beautiful person whose criticism was so devastating because it was so true and so needed, and hence, at the time, so unwelcome—criticism that has spurred you to a lifetime of continued learning, learning year after year what your teachers taught you. Yes, time, and deepening maturity and understanding, will call up an awareness of what your teachers are doing for you.

What of today? How much are you aware of the hours and hours of devotion and care for you that are gifts from your teachers? Pushing and praising, demanding, supporting, nudging, suggesting, explaining and entertaining, hoping for your increasing success—these are some of the thoughtful ways of helping you that occur every day. How much can you see? How often are you looking, with this in mind?

One Sunday in January I was listening to classical music on a Boston FM station. The announcer reported that Jules Eskin, the distinguished cellist who was to have been a guest during the morning, would not appear. "Eskin," said the announcer, "has to practice some of the pieces which he will be playing this afternoon."

Eskin, as many of us know, has been first cello in the Boston Symphony for many years and is one of the finest cellists in the world. That afternoon he was to play in Cambridge with the Boston Symphony Chamber Players, the group that appeared in Memorial Hall a year ago. An experienced, talented cellist; no doubt thoroughly familiar with everything that was to be played that afternoon. Yet he wanted to practice, and so he could not come to the studio to be interviewed. What high standards true artists set for themselves!

Your teachers have high standards for themselves, too. Many enjoyed hours of relaxation during the spring vacation, but I know no one was far from a book, or many books, at any time. Minds while relaxing are also turning to the work ahead, reviewing, analyzing, planning, moving on in thoughts for work with you in the coming weeks of this term.

You are fortunate in the exciting talents of your teachers, and in their devotion to you. I hope you will recognize how much your teachers are doing for you and with you.

And I hope you will express your appreciation to them every now and then. You should. You will be better if you do so. Your teachers will be embarrassed, and they will say, "Yes, yes, of course, of course, thank you." But your expression of gratitude will mean much to them.

"A beautiful teacher.... An impossible person.... Criticism that was devastating.... But, twenty-one years later, I am still learning what he taught me."

Wisdom and knowledge and learning we will value above sceptre and throne. It is through others that the spirit of wisdom comes to each of us. And we are grateful.

Let us pray.

"God grant that I may speak according to his will, and that my own thoughts may be worthy of his gifts; for even wisdom is under God's direction, and he corrects the wise; we and our words, prudence, and knowledge and craftsmanship, all are in his hand." Amen.

—*Chapel Talk, April 4, 1976*

Visitation

No policy issue in the middle years of Bill's rectorship aroused more passions than what he termed "visitation," the circumstances (if any) in which boys and girls could be present in each other's dormitory rooms— a privilege that had been forbidden at St. Paul's since the advent of coeducation. For some concerned faculty and parents, the idea raised "the ugly specter of illicit sex," as history teacher Roberta E. C. Tenney would memorably phrase it in a report on the question. For most students, "parietals" (another term, derived from the Latin word for "wall," which some Catholic universities used to describe the privilege of coed visiting hours) seemed only a natural extension of the many ways in which gender integration at St. Paul's was taken for granted in the daily life of the school, just five years after the implementation of coeducation. For Bill it was a thorny issue but, above all, one to be approached holistically, with due regard for the natural developmental realities. Whatever his personal feelings, he was determined to maintain a neutral position on any new policy as the school reviewed the issue.

So, as he did with most matters, Bill approached the question methodically, knowing it would have to be resolved somehow if the school were fully to embrace coeducation's implications of mutual respect and regard between the sexes. As he describes in this charming recollection, excerpted from a talk delivered in 1996 to mark the twenty-fifth anniversary of coeducation at St. Paul's, he chose to resolve the matter by talking it to death—in a seemingly endless series of studies, committees, reports, and communiqués. The result? Visitation was ultimately adopted without so much as a whisper of controversy. The new policy worked so smoothly that, shortly after its adoption, the student newspaper, the Pelican, *ran a cartoon of a worried Bill, gazing skyward at clouds labeled "ugly specter" and "bad P.R." with a furled umbrella in his hand, while a single raindrop plopped down behind him, unnoticed. And though subsequent administrations would revise and refine (and, in some ways, restrict) the privilege, it remains an accepted and largely unquestioned aspect of school life.*

THE WORD "VISITATION" connotes for St. Paul's School a situation in which students may enter and be in dormitories of the opposite sex. Boys in girls' dormitories; girls in boys' dormitories. In the hallways, in the common rooms, and in the dormitory rooms. The Winter Term of 1971, when girls first arrived, had begun without visitation.

I must tell you of my good fortune in watching coeducation unfold. When I had moved into the rectory, I had constructed a small study on the second floor of the rectory, on top of the library. This area previously had been an unheated sun porch. From my desk I looked out on the Corner House, the flagpole, the center of the school—a wonderful perch from which to watch the busy crossroads of school life.

You may remember that the first nineteen girls were housed in Corner. Immediately I noticed that the traffic in this area picked up, and at the same time slowed down. All day, but especially just before breakfast. At a quarter of seven, along would come a boy, kicking a stone which always seemed to get lost in the snow or grass, necessitating a time-consuming search. Other boys would give close inspection to the bricks in the path, or the work of the snowplow. The boys were hoping that, just by chance, a girl would emerge from Corner and they could walk with her to the Upper for breakfast.

One morning, at eleven minutes before seven, a boy arrived and waited nervously outside the Corner door. One minute early for his ten of seven date. At nine minutes before seven (suitably late one minute), a girl came out, and the two headed for the Upper, happily talking. Imagine it! A date for breakfast at the Upper at ten minutes before seven. What would the students and faculty of the 1890s have said?

I have often been asked, when was the first time a boy or girl mentioned to you how much better the school would be if only boys could go into girls' dormitories? And vice versa. My answer is that I think it was about 2 P.M. on January 3, 1971, the day the girls arrived, when this question was first asked of me. It might have been ten that morning, I can't be sure of the exact time. But I do know that it was early on, very early, in our coeducational life.

As the months rolled on, the question was asked from time to time. An article appeared in the *Pelican*, followed by an editorial. It was now 1972 and 1973. The word "visitation" began to appear on the agenda of Student Council meetings—at first as the last item, never reached, then gradually working its way toward the top, and receiving recognition and attention. More articles appeared in the *Pelican*. More editorials. Finally, a survey by students of practices in other schools. Then a committee study sponsored by the Student Council and the *Pelican*. With interest and attention building, a committee of students and faculty, appointed by me, finally appeared in the fall of 1975.

All of these *Pelican* articles and editorials and Council discussions and surveys and committee discussions had one thing in common: they agreed with that first questioner of January 3, 1971. Yes, the school would be a better place with visitation. Now.

In March 1976 I spoke in the chapel, responding to the recommendations of the committee I had appointed. Everyone expected the start of visitation. My judgment that day was that there were additional productive things we could do, to achieve further social learnings and understandings, that would help ensure the success of visitation when we finally introduced it. I knew of course that it would be a disappointment to many not to have visitation commence that day. How much of a disappointment? Could the school accept another period of waiting?

My normal schedule included weekly meetings, on Thursday afternoons, with the psychologists and the psychiatrist, during which we talked extensively about the general state of the school. These meetings were never more important to me and to the School than in the Winter Term of 1976.

It was my judgment that the school would go along with my two conclusions: first, the formation of the study group, of which I shall speak in a moment; second, my categorical statement that visitation was coming soon. I said, "I believe we shall find a way, through further consideration and work together, in which visitation can be a fact and become a positive personal experience for students. . . . I believe that day will come." This statement did much to ensure the cooperative acceptance of what many perceived to be an unnecessary further delay in establishing visitation.

In April 1976, at the start of the Spring Term, I established the study group of eleven members: three students; two faculty spouses; four faculty members, including Virginia Deane, one of our first and finest female teachers; Dr. Emery, the consulting psychiatrist; and myself as chairman. I asked the group to meet as frequently as possible to discuss the meaning and implications of visitation for the school.

During the Spring Term of 1976, the study group met over luncheon in Scudder on many Tuesdays and Thursdays, seven meetings in all. One meeting, at 5 P.M. here in Memorial Hall, was open to everyone. The editor of the *Pelican* was invited to attend all meetings as a nonparticipant observer.

Discussions were tape recorded. The transcripts of each discussion were typed, anonymously (that is, without attributing names to comments). Copies were made available to everyone for reading: five copies on reserve in the library, three copies with the rector's secretary in the

Schoolhouse, three copies in the faculty room. Each study group member also received a copy, as did the Student Council. Everyone in school—students, faculty, spouses, staff—was invited to read these papers, to keep up with the progress of deliberations by the study group, and to give suggestions and comments to group members.

In late May I announced that the transcripts would be printed in a booklet, and that the booklets would be sent, early in the summer, to students and parents for reading during the summer months. In addition to the transcripts, the report included a letter I had sent on March 11 to all parents, five chapel statements made in previous weeks, and a six-page letter from me, written to facilitate reading and understanding (a "how to read this report" letter).

The study group report was also sent in June to faculty and their spouses, to all new students entering in the fall and their parents, to officers, directors, and representatives of the St. Paul's School Alumni Association, and to members of the Board of Trustees. No one escaped. Everyone associated with the school now knew we were heading for visitation.

The Fall Term began in September 1976 without visitation so that dormitories could discuss the report of the study group. I asked that these deliberations include everyone associated with the dormitory: resident faculty; the third faculty person, nonresident, now working with each dormitory; faculty spouses; the student council representative; all the students.

Looking toward the advent of visitation, I said it was my intention, in time, to make two general school-wide policy statements. First, visitation could take place daily between 9 A.M. and 10 P.M., seven days a week. Second, the date visitation would begin. All further details concerning the management of visitation in dormitories would be determined by those living in the dormitory and associated with it. I asked that discussions of the study group's report be carried on with this important responsibility in mind.

Further, I said, when members of a dormitory had discussed the issues developed in the study group report sufficiently, and felt ready to manage visitation in their house, a letter should be written to me, signed by faculty, the student council representative, and the elected house leaders, so stating. When all dormitories had notified me, visitation would begin.

It took a month before the first dormitory letter reached me. You may think that was a long time, but schools are busy places, and everyone has much to do. Gradually, all dormitories reported, and visitation began.

It is interesting to recall some of the dormitory decisions. Two dormitories concluded that they would not have any visitation at all. One dormitory decided on a half hour a day, from 2 P.M. until 2:30 P.M. Some allowed visitation from the beginning to the end of the day, that is from 9 A.M. until 10 P.M., the maximum allowable amount. There were other patterns. Each dormitory decided what was comfortable for itself, and what it wanted to try to manage.

The next year, September 1977, also began without visitation, as did subsequent years. Each fall the dormitories were asked to have discussions of the issues involved in visitation, based on the study group report, informing the rector when they were ready. School-wide, this process took five or six weeks. Visitation would begin some time the middle or end of October.

How did visitation go? How did coeducation go?

In 1981 St. Paul's School celebrated the 125th anniversary of its founding, with many activities, including a dance, a big cake, a buggy ride recalling the arrival of the first rector and his wife. To mark the occasion in a scholarly way, we sponsored and commissioned two issues of *Daedalus*, the journal of the American Academy of Arts and Sciences. These journal articles, covering issues of importance in American public and private education in the late 1970s, were written by scholars from all over the country. For example, Myron Atkin, dean of the Stanford Graduate School of Education, wrote an essay entitled "Who Will Teach in High School?" reviewing conditions as women began to move away from long-held patterns into professional careers in law, business, and medicine.

In addition to the essays on broad topics, the editor of *Daedalus*, Steve Graubard, and I had decided there should be reports by trained observers on visits to three different kinds of American schools: a public high school (the one chosen was in downtown Atlanta), an independent day school (a suburban school in Chicago was selected) and an independent boarding school (St. Paul's). Two prominent educators, Sarah Lawrence Lightfoot of Harvard and Philip W. Jackson of the University of Chicago, spent six days at each of the three schools. Then, without consulting each other, they wrote an essay about each school.

As part of the 125th anniversary celebration, the Board of Trustees also commissioned a history of the school, to be written by August Heckscher, then a member of the board, and an alumnus of many years' association with the school.

As a result, in 1981 we had three written statements about the school at the end of ten years of coeducation. (I would add that these three statements are available for reading today.)

These three contemporaneous reports describe a busy, happy school. The number of applicants for admission had increased strikingly, as did the yield, the percentage of admitted candidates accepting places. Heckscher wrote that "St. Paul's in the late 1970s could be viewed as a kind of modern utopia," a theme also adopted by Jackson, whose previous experiences had been almost entirely with struggling public schools.

The remarkable thing to me, in reading these two sociological studies and the alumnus history, is that the word "visitation" is not mentioned. Also remarkable, there are few references to coeducation. The observers had seen a school not marked by gender differences. A community of busy, productive students and faculty.

Sara Lightfoot attended Anniversary and Graduation in June 1981, arriving Friday morning and staying until late Sunday afternoon. She attended the symposium on Saturday morning in Memorial Hall, a two-hour meeting during which, each Anniversary, statements by students were given, followed by general discussion stimulated by questions from alumni and parents attending the session.

As she closed her *Daedalus* essay, Lightfoot quoted from one of the student's speeches:

> As males and female living together, day by day, we see each other both at our strongest and at our most vulnerable moments. We encounter each other in the classroom—and at breakfast. Superficiality cannot survive fried eggs in the morning. Casual, regular interaction compels a better knowledge of ourselves. In my personal experience here at St. Paul's, I have seen a great change in my own ways of thinking, one that I had not been consciously aware of, but a change that I had taken for granted. In my first year I tended to think of people in distinct male or female roles. Now I realize by encountering people in a coeducational setting that I must free them to be individuals, free them to develop the full spectrum of human responses and potential.

Finally, a concluding paragraph from Lightfoot's essay:

> To a visitor, the girls at St. Paul's seem fully integrated into the setting. They are serious athletes, sensitive artists, bright and inquiring students, aggressive journalists, and student leaders. In ten years the comfortable assimilation of girls into the historically all-male environment appears to have been accomplished.

I commend the students and faculty of the '70s. I salute coeducation at St. Paul's. Thank you.

—1996

Ambiguity

Over his years of study, Bill was deeply influenced by such educational scholars as Erik Erikson, Jean Piaget, David McClelland, and especially William G. Perry Jr., an educational psychologist and his mentor at the Harvard Graduate School of Education. Perry famously studied college students' progression from strict dualist thinking—based on inviolate notions of "right" and "wrong," dispensed by "good" or "bad" authorities— to an acceptance of multiple, conflicting versions of truth, representing plausible, legitimate alternatives (not all of them equally valid or wise).

It is understandable enough that Bill should have found practical merit in such thinking as he took the helm of St. Paul's in 1970, at a turbulent time in the life of the school and the nation. He knew that St. Paul's would have to change or wither. To put it mildly, such concepts were alien—if not revolutionary—to the way the school had seen itself for decades. There were inevitably bumps along the road, and indeed, some future rectors would come to take a less open approach to such questions (with varying degrees of success). But Bill's own tenure seemed only to buttress his belief in the value—yes, even the necessity—of living with ambiguity. In this talk to the faculty at the start of his next-to-last school year as rector, Bill explains his views in what can also be read as a summing up of his entire administration.

133

I AM GOING TO SPEAK this morning on the subject of ambiguity, on the role of the ambiguous in modern society—in St. Paul's School.

I do so for several reasons. First, I know that for some of the faculty in past school years my references to ambiguity have been confusing—in some instances, maddening, I am told. At various times in the past I have been advised by friends: never use the word "ambiguous" or the word "ambiguity" again in describing actions or thoughts or objectives. I have not followed this advice, as many of you have recognized.

But I have been aware that people are sometimes uncomfortable with my devotion to ambiguity. And it has seemed appropriate, therefore, to me, for some time, to make a statement to you that would place my views on ambiguity in a larger context, an educational and philosophical context, so that this seeming personal predilection of mine could be understood as a wise, mature philosophical belief.

Such is one reason for my decision to speak on the ambiguous this morning. But there are other reasons. I have wondered myself about this personal predilection. I have been traveling along for some time, guided in this important respect, by an intuitive force, a gut feeling. A predilection, the dictionary states, is a preference "often performed as the result of personal leanings or disposition, rather than from objective knowledge." What objectivity? What knowledge can be found if I could spend some time thinking and reading on the matter, to explain and support my "personal leanings or disposition"? In short, I was curious myself. Curious to discover where all of this came from, its meaning and its relationship to important things in our life together.

What you will hear this morning, therefore, is the result of my reading and thinking this summer as I have tried to draw together concepts and influences and hopes that have been around for quite a while. There are several things about me that you are aware of. And I want to reassure you that I am aware of these things also—principally, in this context, things that I am not.

I am not a trained philosopher. I am not a trained educational theorist. I have, of course, been exposed to philosophy. And, I have been exposed to educational theory. I can recognize from both sources the twin influences of stimulus and pragmatic caution.

My statement is not one of theory and philosophy, tightly defined. It is rather a series of speculations and affirmations that produce, in toto, a feeling of improved understanding for myself of the context of ambiguity. I state deliberately "a feeling of improved understanding," even though for you this may be a contradiction in terms. For me it is not.

I have the hope that this will have a similar helpfulness for you. Please allow me to have this hope. It is what keeps me going! I have the hope, at the very least, that having heard my statement, you will have an improved understanding of the meaning of ambiguity for me.

Here we go: "Ambiguous. Admitting more than one interpretation, or explanation."—*The Oxford English Dictionary*.

How important in human affairs is the concept of clarity? To be clear and precise in describing issues, even very complicated matters, is said to guarantee understanding in relationships among people. And true understanding has an inner powerful force that will achieve agreement in the description of issues. This agreed-upon understanding, finally, will result in amicable acceptance of complicated human matters as the basis for resolution of sharp differences among competing peoples or groups.

Clarity of thought and clarity of expression, therefore, have long been considered significant abilities to be learned during school days, and to be employed thereafter in human affairs. These objectives have always characterized educational activity in St. Paul's School. They are pursued today in the study of every course in the curriculum, for critical analysis, initially, is developed equally in almost all study: in considering complicated social situations, viewed in history courses; in testing obscure, sometimes experimental writing in foreign languages, both ancient and modern, and in English; in judging intent and achievement in the fine arts, in drama, music, dance, painting, or in any of the other visual arts; and, in fact, in the study of most, probably all, subjects in the academic curriculum. In these and in other studies, students learn clarity in thinking and in expression, achieving capacities and abilities that follow scholarly traditions common in Western civilization for centuries.

It is a matter worth considering and inquiring about to note that clarity and precision do not permeate all aspects of school life. In many, perhaps most, areas of personal relationships, the efforts of students and faculty unite in seeking goals that are well described, but the ways through which those goals are to be achieved are left undefined and ambiguous. For example, the school leaves members of the faculty free to teach in ways they find effective and comfortable.

Some departments work toward a certain cohesion by placing a common final examination before all students who are studying a subject. And the examination is then graded jointly by the four or five teachers who have taught sections of that subject during the year. In other departments, teachers develop examinations only for their own sections, grading them by themselves so that final testing of the work of the year follows with consistency the daily and weekly patterns established by the individual teacher.

Furthermore, no common patterns are established in coaching terms, for advising student activities, in the handling of tables at seated meals in the dining room, or in advising students in dormitories. Characteristics of personal interest, professional training, experience, age, and individual preference are important in determining the array of specific responsibilities a member of the faculty will have. And this in turn accounts for substantial diversities in the expectations the school has for each faculty member and, necessarily therefore, a particular evaluative consideration for each will obtain.

In similar ways the school accords a considerable latitude for personal choice to students in reaching important decisions in their lives. Many academic subjects are offered, at many levels of competence, with the result that no two students will have identical schedules. Or, if they do, the explanation will be coincidence and personal desire rather than external compulsion.

Diploma requirements, broadly stated, ensure each student's introductory study in all major scholarly fields, while affording opportunity for substantial investigation and beginning mastery in several areas; further, the requirements expect an advanced level of competence in one or two studies.

The Independent Study Program affords a culminating experience for students in their sixth form year, fashioning a pattern of academic and nonacademic activity suited to their interests and abilities, free of specific school direction save the requirements that what is chosen provide opportunity for worthwhile learning, and that the learning be accomplished with the greatest degree of excellence possible.

In other areas of school life a student must make decisions of considerable importance in daily living, without a set of detailed guidelines from the school. When should study take place? What time should study begin in the evening? Should it be in the library or in the dormitory, or somewhere else? What time to go to bed, and what time to get up in the morning? What time to eat, save evening seated meals? Or whether to eat at all, at cafeteria meals, particularly breakfast, and most particularly breakfast during the dark winter mornings? What athletics to choose each term, or whether to choose sports at all during sixth form year? What activities to join and support? Finally, the broadest question of all, and the most significant: what should be the balance of time and energy accorded to study, athletics, activities, and the desire and need to talk to others? Each student may have discussions with friends and faculty about personal questions and personal philosophy, about questions of the greatest importance: the meaning of life, the meaning of my life, of my world; what am I doing in my world, and what should I look forward to, what should I work toward?

In earlier days a school structure provided answers in many of these areas. Three meals a day, at precise times, were required. Everyone played football and hockey; almost everyone rowed in the spring. Monitored study halls called for study at specific times, or at least presence in the study hall, save for the occasional excused time to get a haircut or to take a bath. Activities took place Thursday evenings in rigidly defined societies: Cadmean, Concordian, Library, Scientific Association, and others. Class scheduling was by form section, identical for each group of twelve, offering one science, one history, one mathematics, religious studies, and so on.

Services in the chapel present a sharp contrast today to those of earlier times, both in frequency and in the planning and substance of the services. Until ten years ago required morning chapel daily, and several services on Sunday, were conducted by members of the Sacred Studies Department, ordained ministers of the Episcopal Church, in close consonance with the liturgical and theological beliefs and practices of the church. Participation by lay members of the school, faculty or student, was rare, and limited to contributing within the framework of the expectations of the church.

Today, attendance by students and faculty is expected only at four morning chapel services each week (Monday, Tuesday, Thursday, Friday). Planning for these services is the responsibility of the Chapel Vestry, a group of ten or twelve students who have volunteered, along with one or two faculty members, under the general guidance of the school chaplain, who is also the head of the Religion Department. Some services are conducted following the liturgy of the Episcopal Church; some are devoted to the reading of passages from the Bible, as in earlier days. Such reading is now introduced by a statement of four or five minutes, written by the reader, usually a student, discussing the principal meaning of the passage to be read, a practice that ensures reasonably close attention from the entire school. The majority of morning chapel services today, however, follow other patterns: musical performance by a small group or by an individual; a skit or short play, sometimes presented by a class; a message interpreted by dance; a short address or statement by a student or a lay member of the faculty; a brief sermon by one of the school ministers.

Another part of the life of the school where precision and clarity are lacking is the broad area of human relationships thought of in the mention of the word "discipline." What happens when a student fails to live within major school rules? The rules themselves are clear enough, and they are frequently stated for all to see: first, in a printed *Student Handbook*, distributed to all students. The rules are read to the entire school in the first meeting in the fall and again in the first evening dormitory meeting;

and the statement is posted on bulletin boards throughout school buildings. The major rules are these: Students must do their own work. They may not drive cars in Concord or in surrounding areas except with specific permission. Gambling and explosives are not allowed. No use or possession of drugs, including alcohol. The use of tobacco is allowed only with written parental permission for fourth, fifth, and sixth formers, and only at times and places as announced.

In the view of some, the situation following the failure of a student to live in accord with these rules presents an opportunity for a direct, forthright response. Breaking this rule should have this punishment, and so on. In this view, clarity and precision should prevail. There should be no ambiguity. But this has not been our practice. Rather, our efforts in such situations have been directed toward understanding fully the circumstances of the incident, and also toward understanding the student and his motivation; that is, what within him, rather than without, has led him to this particular action.

There are many educational reasons for this policy, which I discussed in some detail in my letter to alumni in the Fall 1978 issue of the *Alumni Horae*. Here I call attention only to the fact that clarity and precision are deliberately lacking, as in other situations already mentioned, in our work with the behavior of students, particularly in disciplinary matters.

Why? Why is this so? Why are so many issues confronting students and faculty left open for their choice and final decision, issues which in earlier years at the school were settled definitively by school policy that was clearly stated? What accounts for the substantial changes that have occurred in the educational climate and social customs, in the administration, of St. Paul's School?

In responding to these questions, one thinks first of the many changes that have taken place in American society and in Western, indeed world, culture, since the end of the Second World War. Challenges to authority and to orthodoxy have arisen throughout the world, provoking sweeping and fundamental change in patterns followed previously for hundreds of years. Reflected today in the school society—that is, students and faculty and their families and alumni and parents and friends, drawn from almost every state in the nation and from many foreign countries—are a diversity of views and a pluralism of belief that constitute St. Paul's School almost as a world society.

No longer is the school a quiet shadow of the East, of New York, Philadelphia, and the Atlantic coast, of the church, of a society relatively closed, with primarily parochial interests and concerns. The school has marched into and has been swept along by the deep currents of change that have transformed the modern world, most particularly in enshrining a strong spirit of independence critical of authority.

In such a society one asks not only what efforts should be sustained in a small enclave of life (the school) to maintain a resolute authoritarian direction, but also the even more telling question: is resolute authoritarian direction possible at all? Or desirable?

Is it a plausible expectation to administer any portion of society today with the concepts of leadership prevalent only a short time ago? Is it possible to fashion an orthodoxy of values and educational belief that would embrace the numerous divergencies in points of view found in our world today?

Furthermore, what would be the cost in the dampening of freshness and in restricting creativity if a precise and clear orthodoxy prevailed in the selection of faculty and in the reward system for teaching activities? Or, perhaps of greater significance, what would be the cost in restricting the selection of students to those who would appear to be most inclined toward obedient, docile behavior within clearly defined patterns? What would be the cost in containing the educational experiences of students during three or four years within a tight system of values and educational objectives? With a diploma in hand, where would such graduates go in a world filled with ambiguity, to discover another society with simple and precise expectations and customs?

These considerations alone, however, do not explain satisfactorily or account fully for the change in school policies that have placed the responsibility for making numerous decisions in the hands of faculty and students. That is, the growing influence of diversity and pluralism as social forces and the difficulty of maintaining an authoritarian atmosphere in school life only define the conditions of society within which educational policies and objectives can be determined. Some institutions—schools, colleges, others—continue to attempt to achieve precision and clarity in defining the expectations held for the actions of members of their group, apparently finding other important gains to balance what appears to be an enormous cost to the individuals in restrictions on their freedom of activity and development.

Why then has such a fundamental change taken place at St. Paul's School? Why has this educational philosophy appeared at St. Paul's, if indeed this is not an automatic or necessary part of a widespread development in education generally?

It is of course open to those responsible for an institution to decide that change, even fundamental change, must be introduced into the relationships of its members. For St. Paul's School, in 1970, such a decision was reached when I decided to introduce, carefully but with consistent intent, the concepts of what is broadly termed developmental education. Substantial achievements in studies in sociology, anthropology, psychiatry, and general psychology since the Second World War had pointed to new directions in emphasis for guidelines for school activities. The writings and work of many scholars, especially Piaget, Erikson, McClelland, and Perry, influenced this decision in significant ways. In particular, the encouragement which I have received for many years from William G. Perry Jr. of Harvard was of the greatest importance to me. Professor Perry's experimental work, concerning the changes in patterns of thinking which occur in the late adolescent years, provided a continuing source of stimulus and a continuing note of pragmatic caution. Both influences were needed and were received as welcome support when understandings were incomplete, as new relationships among students and faculty were experienced.

Since 1970, therefore, we as a school have sought to understand these emerging educational philosophies and to determine how and in what ways they could be introduced productively and effectively into secondary education. The effect of this effort has been to add a new direction to the school's sense of purpose while maintaining carefully all of the traditional objectives long associated with St. Paul's. A new attention has been accorded to the individual, both faculty and student, with the intention and hope of fostering and stimulating personal growth and development. Teaching and learning have become inextricably interwoven, with emphasis for faculty on the opportunity to continue learning while teaching, and for students on the opportunity to teach while learning. These general goals have been pursued in explicit ways: in developing classroom procedures, methods, and activities; in providing guidance for the sharing of work undertaken by faculty and students in dormitories and in school activities generally; and, most important, in participation in the responsibilities of reaching decisions as extensively as possible in the administrative leadership of the school.

Traditional objectives have not been neglected, meanwhile. The achievement of excellence continues to be sought in studies long associated with Western civilization: mathematics, history, science, religion, and in writing, the understanding and use of the English language, and ancient and modern foreign languages. Our continuing success in the record of admission of graduates to highly competitive colleges (mentioned later in this statement) attests to the attainment of this important part of the educational endeavor.

In addition, study and teaching and participation in the fine arts, for credit and for pleasure, have been broadened to include dance, drama, and music, as well as the many forms of the visual arts. Participation in sports and games contributes to a general understanding of the health of the body, providing a base for occasional school-wide attention to such significant matters as sleep and rest, nutrition, exercise, weight control, and the use of stimulants. The Independent Study Program, as mentioned earlier, provides opportunities for testing the nonacademic world during and throughout the sixth form year, in activities that must be carefully identified, developed, and monitored.

There remains one broad objective of the school to mention, that of fostering a sense of community. Since the earliest days, association with the school has brought to faculty and students a feeling of belonging, and of having belonged, to a community where each individual knows every other individual. Caring for others has characterized to a remarkable degree every person in the place. There is no doubt that the size of the school, always small enough to make this possible, has fostered this feeling. Certainly the school's location in the relative isolation of central New Hampshire severely limited opportunities for involving people or groups from the outside in school life, until the interstate highways and the automobile and bus in recent years brought much of New England within easy reach.

There are historical roots, then, for the feeling of community which now so permeates all relationships in school life. Recent developments in the years since the end of the Second World War have brought two counterbalancing forces. On the one hand, modern technology in communication and transportation has injected national and world influences into the school society, thus reducing the intensity of the focus of students and faculty on local matters. On the other hand, interest in the lives of other people has been fostered in many ways in the larger society: through the growth of the influence of social and religious movements; through dangers to the very existence of human life perceived to come from modern scientific developments and bitter national rivalries; through the appearance and exploitation of "causes" by leaders whose strident activities often dominate national attention.

The resulting accommodation of these forces—interest in others, historically part of the life of the school, intensified by social and cultural movements that are worldwide—has provided a receptive atmosphere for work with individuals and groups. In study in small classes, sometimes through individual counseling, carefully directed by well-trained and experienced psychologists, students have learned much about themselves. They have had opportunities to explore small changes in their relationships with others within sympathetic groups of friends. In coming to understand some of the forces within themselves that help explain their own attitudes and their own reactions to situations and to other people, students have developed in turn an appreciation of the forces that lie behind the lives of others, their friends and loved ones.

And these understandings have led to greater acceptance both of themselves and of others, and of social situations. Actions understood through awareness of the forces lying beyond the surface of visible activity become actions accepted through the mediating bonds of human love and compassion. Finally, students have learned that, occasionally, actions must be accepted in reluctant resignation, as necessary, even though the situation is not understood and is not wanted.

Students talk about these matters lengthily, almost endlessly, in discussions with each other, in confidential meetings with faculty, in the setting of confidential group meetings, in essays and papers in their English course work, in poetry, drama, and essays composed for school publications and competitions. They talk about existence and the issues of the origin and continuance of life. They are concerned with the major existential questions that have always confronted mankind: the meaning of life and the world; the importance of the individual; issues of determinism; and the significance of individual human life. And they have learned that the answers to such questions are beyond the realm of certitude.

But students have also learned in their studies that final and exact certitude lies beyond even the ultimate revelations of modern science and philosophy and other studies. They have learned that men and women today, in spite of impressive accumulations of knowledge and accomplishments, are yet short of final understanding of many significant questions, and that such has always been the case even though, through the centuries, the known and apparently certain have grown enormously.

For students, an influence of considerable significance at this point is the general atmosphere of the school itself: the prevailing attitudes toward authority and certainty and ambiguity. The experience for students of having participated in a search for satisfactory solutions to community situations, knowing that the best response is not usually immediately available, has pointed the way toward the need to tolerate moments in which clarity and precision are absent, or at least not present to the degree that at any given time one might wish were the case. It is not a surprise, nor is it a shock, then, for students to discover that the answers to the major questions confronting human beings, as they struggle to make meaning of their lives, have not been definitely established in philosophy or religion. Students have observed by this time a way of considering various opinions within uncertainty, as the school has sought to use the best thoughts of many people in reaching a decision on a matter that will be positive and productive for both the individuals who are involved and for the community itself.

And, at this time, students also realize the important influence of the strong church traditions of the school, of classroom experience in religious studies, and of regular presence, week after week, month after month, at morning services in the school chapel. What can one believe? Can one move beyond belief to faith? Is there reason enough to hope? Is there enough hope and faith to justify going on? How does one find a life of productive and worthwhile accomplishment?

These are not, of course, simple questions. Nor are they simple matters. But they are the issues encountered in late adolescence, and they are the questions that must be answered satisfactorily if life is to be lived on a level that is not only chronologically adult but adult in wise maturity, in clear knowledge of the many uncertainties and ambiguities that existence entails.

—*Faculty Meeting, September 7, 1980*

The Arts in Education

From his earliest days at the school—and perhaps influenced by his own interdisciplinary undergraduate studies—Bill believed that the arts were not a tertiary or discretionary aspect of the educational experience, but central to the creation of a learned person. As rector he made study of the arts a mandatory part of the curriculum, and by the mid-1970s he began to press—successfully in the end—for significant new spaces for the practice and performance of music, dance, and drama. These spaces would physically transform the heart of the school grounds and greatly reshape the parameters of a St. Paul's education in ways felt deeply to this day, not least in his name on the bricks and mortar at the center of the new space.

"I AM HUMBLE with designers," remarked Armi Ratia, creator of Marimekko. "I tell them, 'Find yourself.' Then it works."

When we contemplate the study of the arts at St. Paul's School, we know the arts will help students find themselves in the fullest possible way. We know this is the answer to the question as to why everyone in our world today should become acquainted with music, drama, the dance; with painting, sculpting, drawing, designing, and the many forms of the visual arts.

In the early days of St. Paul's School, and through the years until 1971, students left to make their own decisions could choose only limited work in the arts, to be carried out in their free time without academic credit. As part of a general review of the course of study and of diploma requirements, begun in 1970, decisions providing for substantial changes in emphasis in the curriculum were reached in 1971. Full-year courses, carrying academic credit, were established in the arts for both performance and study, and the successful completion of at least one full year of work in the arts was included in requirements for the school diploma.

As a consequence of this change in emphasis, which included a reduction of required work in other academic departments, the numbers of faculty in some departments declined as professionals in the arts were added to the faculty. Today the faculty has, as full-time members, three instructors in music, four instructors in the visual arts, a director of dance, and a drama instructor. Each department of the arts, furthermore, has part-time instructors to help with specialties. The largest number of part-time assistants, those in the Music Department, thirteen this year, teach the harp, the French horn, and such other instruments requiring particular and unique guidance.

The addition of professionals to the faculty in support of this strong emphasis in the arts has made possible not only the skillful education and development of performers in these varied fields, but also the teaching of courses in history and theory, studies so necessary to inform performance. Some of these courses given each year are: The Theater and the Play; Art History; The Modernist Viewpoint; Music Theory and Composition; Understanding Music; Beethoven and the Romantics Who Followed; Advanced Ballet.

The number of students choosing academic work for credit in the arts has increased substantially since 1971, as figures for the school year 1978–79, given here, indicate clearly: dance, 30; drama, 14; visual arts, 148; music, 99. Without gaining academic credit, 57 students participated in chorus, 29 in band, and 16 in the orchestra. Also, 66 students had weekly lessons in the playing of instruments, without academic credit.

In addition, projects in the arts, carried on through the supervision of the Independent Study Program, allow students to combine personal initiative and ambitious imagination with careful attention to the scholarly history and demands of their activity, and with exacting standards for performance.

The school learns almost daily of interest in the arts through activities and performances having no relation to academic credit. Plays, directed and produced and acted in by students, out of pleasure in their work together, bring enjoyment to the whole community. Coming events—athletic games, debates, club meetings—are announced to the school in various ways; sometimes through a series of posters of moderate size, sometimes through mammoth artistic projects placed over the entire wall of the dining room, to be observed by students and faculty at luncheon. Such messages often are the subject of considerable attention in conversation throughout the school for a day or two, because of their ingenuity in design and composition, and their pleasing use of color and texture and arrangement. No garish sign in Times Square, throughout the years, ever received the concentrated attention of some of these messages. Music performances, occasionally in the dining room at dinner, and with more frequency in morning chapel, where dance also appears, remind students and faculty alike of the devoted attention of their friends to these rewarding pursuits.

Where have these activities been prepared? What facilities have there been, in the past few years, for practice and instruction in music, for dance, and for classes in drama performance and production?

Activities require spaces. St. Paul's School has been fortunate throughout the years in the buildings that have been provided by alumni and friends and trustees to support the many different needs of the school. Some facilities commit the school to fundamental ideals and principles which have guided its life and activities from earliest days: the Old Chapel; the glorious Chapel of St. Peter and St. Paul; the Schoolhouse, the Lower Grounds. Other buildings and spaces have supported educational and physical needs: the Armour Infirmary, the kitchen and dining halls, dormitories, Memorial Hall, Payson and Moore for science and mathematics, ponds for skating and rowing, the Gordon Rink and the Gymnasium, the Power Plant.

Beginning in 1858 with construction of the Old Chapel, each building has been added as a response to a need for space for an activity engaged in by a substantial number of students and faculty. When economic pressures in 1963 spurred the consolidation of the school's three dining halls at the Upper, Hargate (no longer needed as a dining hall) was converted to an Art Center, providing excellent spaces for painting, drawing, photography, three-dimensional form, sculpture, and other visual art forms. And the former dining room became an ample and gracious exhibition hall.

As interest in music, dance, and drama increased, space needs for instruction and practice for small and large productions grew. Music lessons and practice moved into rooms all over the school, from Scudder to the Old Chapel, the Choir Room, and, most frequently, the basement area of Memorial Hall. This basement had been excavated and floored at the time of construction of the building, but it was never developed with the attention to sound and air that interior areas must have if they are to provide adequate conditions for learning. The use of these less-than-satisfactory basement spaces has long been an indication of a serious school need. Meanwhile, intense competition developed, between dance and drama, for the use of the stage in Memorial Hall, a strain on students and faculty that was intensified by the need, for each utilization of the stage, to bring in or take away mirrors, bars, chairs, door frames, and other properties, dependent upon the contemplated use of the stage for a relatively short period of time.

Clearly, the time had arrived in the '70s when flourishing activities in the arts called for dedicated spaces for instruction and practice, and for productions of limited scope. Recognition of this need came through the Fund for SPS, when the Board of Trustees authorized generous support in the construction of three buildings now close to completion. The enthusiastic and appreciative response of students and faculty indicates ever deepening interest in drama, music, and dance, and the continuing quest for mastery as participants move together toward ever greater excellence in individual and group efforts.

St. Paul's School has indeed made a clear commitment to the arts and has therefore provided carefully for work in the arts: through the establishment of a number of new faculty positions; through the building of superb physical facilities; through the decision to grant academic credit for course work; through enthusiastic encouragement to informal activities as the arts have permeated daily school life.

These comments suggest important questions. Why should students at St. Paul's School study the arts? Why should everyone in our world today become acquainted with music, drama, the dance; with painting, sculpting, drawing, designing, and the many forms of the visual arts?

First, we know that interest in the arts has characterized the activities of human beings throughout recorded history. We believe that students should come to know more about those activities through formal study, that they may better understand their own human heritage, to participate in the furthering of that heritage.

The making of pottery and jewelry; the choice of materials for clothing and their design; painting on walls and in churches; the construction and location of cathedrals and homes—in these and countless other activities we see concern and care for color, texture, design, and symbol. In festivals and holiday celebrations we learn of attention for sound and rhythm, for movement, and myth and story. Dances to express joy in the arrival of rain or its cessation; ceremonies to prepare for battle or to recover from it. Religious pageant and ritual, clarifying belief for all to see, and to join, in community participation all are occasions that have stretched ingenuity and group effort.

Just this summer I was amazed to note a vast enlargement and extension of community effort in the Fourth of July parade in Brooklin, a small coastal village far Down East in Maine. Twenty years ago, in the hours just before the parade, four or five floats were hastily assembled, the efforts of only a few people. This summer the parade was a significant community achievement that had twenty-seven floats, each carefully worked on for weeks by many groups in the village. And residents of nearby towns, forty to sixty miles away, came to admire glimpses of history, costumes and properties arranged with sensitive care, and community triumph enjoyed greatly by spectators.

Man has always been moved by an innate aesthetic drive to beautify whatever he was working on: trinkets, clothing, shelter, weapon, art objects, celebrations. An important part of our basic humanity is appreciation for beauty in its many forms and in the relationships of each element to others. Eye joins with mind in directing bodily actions and response which identify personality and being.

A second reason for study and experience in the arts is that knowledge of past human interests and achievements informs and deepens appreciation of the present. And formal study contributes markedly to the fulfillment of the potential appreciation which resides in each of us.

Experience with the arts, through study and apprenticeship, focuses attention on an important part of human relationships. For study of the arts brings young people into the immediate presence of the tension between discipline and freedom, of the matter of standards, of taste, of human judgment. And, of even greater significance, it teaches that this tension exists in many areas of human existence, and that this has always been so. Students learn the conventions and customs and methods and judgments which have accumulated around an activity in the arts, through study or through apprenticeship. "See the master at work. He is doing what he wants to do." Or so it seems. And then, by working with the master, the student learns the guidelines and conventions which have led to effectiveness in artistic achievement, including some intuitive processes which neither the master nor the student can describe clearly, apart from the activity. Students learn that the master has carefully moderated what he "wants to do" to bring his efforts within those conventions which encompass his craft. Stravinsky, having this tension in mind, described the classical dance as "the triumph of studied conception over vagueness, of the rule over the haphazard."

To understand and appreciate the practice of the arts in our world today, students must become familiar with developments that have swept far beyond classical practice. Practitioners and critics of painting and sculpture, and of the other forms of the visual arts, have not agreed on a single response to the question, What is art? Hence the museum, long considered the final arbiter of the question, now welcomes the work of artists creating in ever-changing styles and manners far beyond conventions that once were uniformly held. Performance—of music, drama, dance—has become the signal of a certain acceptance which renders explanation or justification unnecessary. Resulting judgments are ambiguous as well as uncertain, as critics and observers stand aside in disagreement and confusion. One critic, Harold Rosenberg, writes that the artist of the modernist or postmodernist schools works primarily in essences: "Instead of painting, he deals in space; instead of dance, poetry, film, he deals in movement; instead of music, he deals in sound."

The restless, creative modern artist, furthermore, experiments with the materials of his craft, bursting the confines that once dictated the limits of his working space. Pierre Boulez and his associates work in the Paris Institute to create new instruments of greater capacity to handle twelve-tonal expression than classical instruments are thought to have. How easy it is to overlook or forget the fact that "classical" instruments once were new.

Thus students learn that there is no single or simple answer to the question, What is art? They become acquainted with artistic achievement throughout the years and centuries of man's existence. They come to know eras of strict discipline and convention as well as periods of experimentation and development. Students experience in their own work the tension between discipline and freedom that has forever confronted artist and critic alike. And they appreciate, better than before, that activities of human existence are complex and complicated and ambiguous, not often clear or precise.

A third reason for the study of the arts is found in the application of this point of view to the work and problems of the world today. Questions of overwhelming difficulty and significance confront society and government. What indeed are the world's major problems? Not a simple question, that. And there should not be, and in fact cannot be, easy answers to it. What understanding of progress should we hold as the twentieth century comes to a close? How concerned should we be about the availability of nonrenewable natural resources? With the impact of growing scarcity? With declining world production? Should we assume the driving ambition and curiosity of man will soon find ways to continue "progress" and "world development" as in the past century or two? Is "quality of life" to dominate all concerns? We recognize that this phrase has no uniformly understood or completely satisfactory meaning. What is the image of the future that our world should hold, knowing the very great importance to daily tasks and accomplishments that goals and objectives have in human society?

These are not easy questions to answer or to begin to answer, nor is it easy even to speculate about such questions.

And there are other questions, equally compelling in significance for the world, which must be considered.

Students experienced in the study and practice of the arts are, I think, ready to consider such issues, with benefit for society. For they understand that there are no simple or immediate responses to complicated human situations. They know there are values in taking into account previous experience and dogma and authority, but they realize that opinions and facts must be interpreted through human judgment—their own, involving thought and consideration and interpretations. They are acquainted with the process of speculation, of identifying, through logical analysis and intuition, a range of factors that must be considered. And they understand that they must remain open to each possibility, realizing the dangers involved in narrowing the scope of inquiry if premature emphasis is laid at any one point.

Further, there will be "tacit integration" (to use Michael Polanyi's phrase) of that independence which allows personal decision, through careful attention for sound discipline which guides and informs choice, while allowing unfettered scope for initiative, curiosity, imagination, and originality.

Why should students study art? A fourth and final reason is that work in the arts provides an opportunity for participants to learn about themselves. This opportunity is particularly valuable for students at St. Paul's School, because it allows, and in some ways demands, consideration of fundamental issues through observation and testing and experimentation. From fourteen years old through eighteen, this chance is eagerly sought and required. This is the period of questioning and exploring, of self-doubt and braggadocio, the period of developing self-confidence and maturing personality. In the arts are found cultural contradictions and conflicts, insight, informed speculation, traditions and discipline, and a general pattern for testing achievement and apparent success. The arts afford the use of uncommitted space for thoughtful and considered growth through consolidation of experimentation. And increasing knowledge of the self promotes and supports its realization.

Ratia's advice to designers, noted above, was first to find themselves, and thereafter successful work in design would be anticipated. "Whoever undertakes to create soon finds himself engaged in creating himself," wrote Harold Rosenberg in *The Tradition of the New.* Can "the new" be considered "tradition"? That, in itself, is an arresting thought. Abundant opportunities exist in the arts, while new concepts are being developed, for creative energy to be usefully employed. It is then that openness is considered traditional. Finally, a decision is reached as an act of affirmation, acknowledging and embracing risk.

One summer night in London in 1975, Pierre Boulez talked of teaching a group of experienced musicians. He had asked each member of the class to compose a short piece while adhering closely to a set of strict musical rules that he formulated for them. Boulez expected the compositions of the different individuals to be quite similar. But they were not, and at first he was puzzled.

Then he gradually came to realize that each composition was in fact a statement and reflection of the individual composer, more self-expression than a response to a specific assignment. Restrictions placed upon the musicians, though defining to some degree the nature of their work, had not blocked the insistent internal drive each had felt for self-exploration in completing this composition exercise.

In the same manner, students develop understandings about themselves based upon the responses of others and painful examination of themselves. Is there a reliable authority to guide and inform these self-judgments? Experiencing some of the joys and frustrations of creation in music or dance, in drama or in the visual arts, prepares our young friends to consider such questions with quiet assurance. For they have already themselves sought a balance between freedom and discipline, between the conventions that organize social judgment and the liberating experimentation that frees the restless quest for more satisfying modes of expression. And they have learned that there is no final satisfying assurance in blind devotion either to the restricting notions of a liturgy or demanding discipline or to the blandishments of totally unstructured freedom.

Hard questions have soft answers, they have learned.

Why should students of St. Paul's School study the arts? Why, indeed, should this annual report be directed to consideration of this question?

Many changes have taken place in St. Paul's School during the past ten years. Those who read about these developments are aware of the increasing prominence of the arts, as instruction and performance have become a large and important part of the life of the school. And they are a part that gives satisfaction to the human spirit, to each individual's sense of creativity. It is important, I think, that friends and alumni know that music and dance and the visual arts and drama are now studied with the rigor and intensity always accorded mathematics and Latin and English, and other subjects long included in our Western educational tradition. And that full academic credit is granted for formal study in the arts.

It is important also, I believe, that I speak of the reasons for these developments and of the relationship of the arts to the philosophy of education which now characterizes the school. The arts have been added to the curriculum, and considerable time and space have been found for arts instruction and performance. But nothing has been taken away. No earlier emphasis has been lessened qualitatively. The school still supports study and mastery in many traditional fields. Alumni and friends, and colleges, know well our emphasis in English, mathematics, modern and ancient languages, religion, history, and the physical sciences. Administrators and teachers in colleges, particularly those working in admissions, should be fully aware of the values of work in our arts program, so that a more accurate picture of our students can be presented and understood. It is my hope that this discussion will serve those important purposes.

—Annual Report of the Rector, 1978–79

Discipline . . . and Ambiguity

Perhaps no concept more consumed Bill—or was more central to the educational philosophy he sought to instill at St. Paul's—than the notion of ambiguity. It is a paradox that a mathematics teacher, and a man of such businesslike mien (at least with facts and figures), should have such a firm and abiding belief in the importance of accepting those aspects of educational endeavor—and indeed of the human experience—in which clarity is lacking. But the idea, developed over many years of study and consideration, was basic to Bill's thinking.

Because the headmaster of an independent boarding school had in Bill's day—and has still at St. Paul's and elsewhere—nearly unchallenged sway over the day-to-day management of the institution, Bill was able to make of St. Paul's a kind of living laboratory in which to test the theories he had absorbed in his years of graduate study at Harvard. As he has noted in other writings, the faculty sometimes saw him as dictatorial and did not accept uncritically his appreciation of ambiguity. Nor, for that matter, did all of the student body. As a somewhat self-righteous and intolerant editor-in-chief of the Pelican, I often called for greater clarity—that is, less ambiguity—especially in matters of discipline. In this Rector's Letter for the Alumni Horae in the autumn of 1978, Bill addresses that issue directly, outlining his views and the foundation for them.

DEAR ALUMNI & ALUMNAE, "What is the educational philosophy behind disciplinary action taken at St. Paul's School?"

My life is filled with unexpected developments. Hence I was not totally surprised to be asked, on Thursday afternoon, September 14, to speak at the faculty meeting the next morning on this broad and very important question. Lead time? A week or two, to gather one's thoughts and put them into sensible order? To confer with colleagues? To write, then edit a statement, and have it edited?

These thoughts went unspoken. For it was clear, in my conversation with the head of the faculty leadership with whom I was speaking, that the moment for me to speak was at hand. Yes, it would have to be the next morning.

What should be the response of a member of the faculty when he or she discovers by chance a student who is breaking one of the School's rules? Students and faculty alike are well aware of these rules, through having heard them read at the first Reports of the year and through reading the *Student Handbook*. Students must do their own work. They may not drive cars in Concord or in surrounding areas except with specific permission. Gambling and explosives are not allowed. No use or possession of drugs, including alcohol. The use of tobacco is allowed with written parental permission for Fourth, Fifth, and Sixth Formers, and then only at times and places as announced.

What is the educational context in which an infraction of a School rule should be viewed? This was the question before me as I composed a statement that Thursday evening. Here is what I said to the faculty, Friday morning, September 15.

My first observation is that we are first and foremost an educational institution, organized and supported for the purpose of helping young students grow and develop, and mature into strong young adults. Our principal activities are controlled by that primary responsibility. Everything we do—our actions and efforts in class, on the athletic fields, in dormitories, in the dining rooms, in activities—every action everywhere is rooted in this primary responsibility. And this includes our actions and responses that are "disciplinary" in nature. Only this Wednesday morning, in Chapel, I had commented that "the lives of teachers . . . are devoted to the care and nurture of experiences and activities in which students can learn." John Dewey used other words, long ago: "Education is precisely the work of supplying the conditions which will enable the psychical functions, as they successively arise, to mature and pass into higher functions in the freest and fullest manner."

It is worth recalling briefly the descriptions of the growth of young people as established in the work of leading philosophers of educational theory. We are working with students who are in what Jean Piaget called the fourth stage, that of rapidly increasing higher levels of logical and cognitive development. This is the era, from age eleven to adulthood, of the development of formal-operational thought: reasoning about reasoning, operations upon operations, true formal thought, the systematic isolation of variables, deductive hypothesis-testing. These and similar activities are the learning processes of our students, the processes to be used and learned. In William Perry's terms, students are passing through upper positions of intellectual and ethical development—from duality to multiplicity, through relativism to commitment—while avoiding alternatives to growth: temporizing, retreat, and escape. We also recall Erik Erikson's concept of maturity: that of fully understanding and accepting oneself, that of fully understanding one's place in time and space, and of accepting that place. These are the essentials of our educational activity as seen through the concepts of three inventive scholars.

Ours is a complex undertaking, far exceeding the demands of earlier eras, which were concerned primarily with straightforward, perhaps simple views of educational objectives. Are we as a faculty in solid agreement about what we should do to insure "the care and nurture of experiences and activities in which students can learn" and grow and develop? No, and far from it. Just as there is no one way to teach mathematics, or history, or any other subject; no single way to coach a soccer team; no one way to interest a table in meaningful conversation at a seated meal. We agree in working toward a common objective. But we work, in each of the many parts of our faculty responsibility, in our own individual and distinctive ways. So with discipline. Broad outlines, general understandings, extended areas of tolerance—these there are. Tight, mandatory, narrow patterns of actions there are not.

Students must adjust, from one year to the next, to different expectations in their subjects as they move from one teacher to another; to varying ways of developing living conditions in dormitories as they move from one dormitory to another, year after year; to varying styles of conducting a table at seated meals. And so on. So, too, are students confronted with varying types of emphasis in their lives and activities, or to use the extreme word, discipline, as they associate with different members of the faculty. We remember, in considering "disciplinary" situations, that human activity is frequently complex, practically never simple, in its motivation. We look as best we are able behind the actions to understand the life of the individual as an indication of the reason for the action. And, again as best we can, our response then is to the controlling forces behind the action, rather than to the action itself.

There does come the time when a student can no longer stay within this environment. That is, he or she can no longer stay in School. Often this is a decision that is simultaneously the best thing for the individual as well as for the School. But in extreme cases the environment, the community, the School, must prevail.

I often think of our experiences with some individuals as a race with time. Will their increasing maturity, their personal strengthening, take place quickly enough, in the face of the private struggle which their lives are, to provide behavior that is acceptable enough for them to continue? Will our patience last? Will the assaults on the community be temperate enough to be acceptable? Will our combined efforts see him or her through to maturity?

If so, what of the specific accomplishments and other actions? What of the High Honors grades or of the team captaincies or of the negatives we could mention? There he stands, a man. There she stands, a woman. Not everyone gets through to maturity in their School years. Some graduate, having run the full course of our School without deviating from a narrow path of activity. Without a personal struggle and without personal accomplishment. If so, the struggle will come in later years.

National surveys indicate that only about fifty percent of the American population ever achieve Piaget's fourth stage. One-half achieve a genuine maturity. The other half spend their adult lives (adult defined here in chronological terms) in a preadolescent state of mental and emotional and perhaps personal development. Staring at the tube, perhaps. So our task is not preordained to success. It is a struggle. We open doors. We look out on vistas. We remove major roadblocks. And we are present as the initiative and interest of the individual student determine how far he or she will travel.

Disciplinary activity, then, is just one part, perhaps a small part, in our total effort to "supply the conditions which will enable the psychical functions ... to mature and pass into higher functions."

These, then, are my thoughts on the educational philosophy behind disciplinary action at St. Paul's School. A quick summary, to be sure, but one I thought of interest to you, to be presented in the pages of our excellent alumni magazine. Parents Day and most of our athletic activities for this term are behind us as I write. Chill is in the air. Can black ice be far behind? I hope not. I send best wishes to each of you from Millville, and my hope that you will visit us frequently, as often as you can.

—*Rector's Letter, Autumn 1978*

Why Was the Last Night Chapel Service So Short?

Bill could be a sentimental man. He sometimes struggled to hold back tears in public speeches when he touched on sensitive topics or tragedies. But he was not one to wear his heart on his sleeve, and in this, his last Rector's Letter to the Alumni Horae, *he reflects with typical emotional economy on the truism of those words in the old hymn: "A thousand ages in thy sight are like an evening gone." It stands as an understated farewell to the institution he had loved and served for forty years.*

DEAR ALUMNI & ALUMNAE, "Mr. Oates, why was the Last Night Chapel Service so short?"

It is Tuesday night, the last night of the Winter Term, and I am sitting in my stall in Chapel at the conclusion of the Last Night Service. Students are filing out as a lively postlude, played on the organ, fills the air. A Fifth Form boy whom I know well comes toward me to say something, and I listen attentively to him as he asks: "Mr. Oates, why was the Last Night Chapel Service so short?"

The question startled me, because the Service had not seemed to me to be short. In fact, it had lasted fourteen minutes. We had sung the traditional "Saviour, Source of

Every Blessing." I had read the Last Night Prayer: "O God, our merciful and gracious Father, in whom we live and move and have our being, we offer thee our humble thanks for all thy loving-kindness and tender mercy. . . ." And so on. We had had other prayers. The Madrigal Singers had sung a lovely motet by Thomas Tallis, and the School Chorus had sung an anthem, "Achieved Is the Glorious Work," by Haydn.

The Service had been as usual: traditional hymns and anthems and prayers. The usual length. But my Fifth Form friend wanted to know why the Service had been so short.

The Last Night Service is one of the most important moments of the year, I think. It is a beautiful, traditional service bringing everyone to a moment of thoughtful and calm reflection. It is a tender moment, too, for it marks a termination of sorts—in this case, the end of the Winter Term. It heralds the end of something, and the start of something else. It is a moment of fragile beauty, of great meaning and significance.

I remembered my Fifth Form friend as a new Third Former: a rollicking, happy-go-lucky boy, carefree and full of fun. And I thought, as he stood there, that it was likely he had not found his first Last Night Service too short. It was too long, without doubt, holding him from the wonderful snowball fights and other spirited fun with friends who awaited him outside the confines of the Chapel as he traveled back to his dormitory.

Time passes. Viewpoints change. New ways of looking at old experiences and events develop and appear.

172

Of change we have had much in these last twelve years. And that is good. But also much remains of the old. And each day I thank our far-sighted Trustees of the 1880s who built our Chapel. And I give thanks also that, as changes have taken place, we have been able to preserve and maintain some of our church traditions, the four required Morning Chapel Services that we have each week, and the other required services we have from time to time, including the Last Night Service.

The changing attitude of this young man instructs us in why we are so fortunate. The normal resistance of youth turns in time to maturity and appreciation. This is the phenomenon we call development. But there must be an arena in which life can be lived. There must be a framework. There must be social demands, rooted in careful thought and evaluation, and hope. The presence of the School, with its aspirations and demands, provides these needed requirements, this framework.

So these years have seen changes: coeducation, a new emphasis on the fine arts, a shifting from education viewed as absolute achievement to a developmental framework, a sharing of the leadership of the School, a concentration and focus on four years of schooling instead of six.

And the years have brought many social changes: informal dress, the possibility of unlimited weekends away from School (a privilege not frequently availed of, because activities at School are so numerous and so pleasant on Saturdays and Sundays); mobility in terms of field trips or excused absences, in numbers staggering to those with long memories who once guarded each and every class period zealously; a practice of absence now well suited to the increased personal responsibility of each student for his and her learning and development. These and many other changes all joining the age-long search and drive for excellence—excellence in writing and understanding languages, both native and foreign; excellence in history and mathematics and science; in the study of ethics and religion, in the fine arts, in athletics, and in all areas of learning in our school.

Our decisions have been purposeful, arrived at after careful consideration. We have kept much of the tradition of the School we have known so long, and we have dropped some few parts that no longer serve. We have considered many changes, and we have adopted some of them.

"Mr. Oates, why was the Last Night Chapel Service so short?" It stirs in me the question, "Mr. Oates, why were these last twelve and a half years so short? Indeed, the last forty?"

And, implicitly, why do they have to come to an end?

This is the way of life, of course. I assure you I leave with some sadness that this part of my life, and this part of the life of the School, are drawing to a close.

But at the same time I am filled with satisfactions: of things attempted, of things achieved, of the support of so many students, so many members of the faculty, and so many alumni, trustees, parents, and friends.

I thank everyone—trustees, faculty, students, alumni, parents, staff, friends—for the wonderfully generous support given to me and to the School these years. It has been my great privilege and honor to serve as Rector, and to be with you.

And now, "May the grace of courage, gaiety, and the quiet mind, with all such blessedness as belongeth to the children of our heavenly Father, be ours, to the praise and glory of his holy Name, both now and for evermore. Amen."

—Rector's Letter, June 11, 1982

Part Four

AT·TWILIGHT

Windsor School Graduation

Bill and Jean retired to Kennebunk on the Maine coast, where he remained highly active, not only in hoeing and weeding his own garden but also in service as an overseer at his beloved Harvard. He was a frequent and erudite writer of letters to the editor of the New York Times *on wildly diverse topics, as one example included here shows. After Jean's death in 2004, he moved to an assisted living community in Westwood, Massachusetts, near the home of his eldest son, Bill. There he remained indefatigable in his intellectual and cultural pursuits, making regular forays to the Boston Symphony, leading discussions on topics of interest for fellow residents, and responding to queries about the composition of this book, as he did in a brief recollection of the philosophy (and eventual practical effects) of his policy on student smoking during his rectorship. Perhaps no duty gave him more pleasure, or engaged him more consistently, than his service as the longtime chairman of his Harvard Class of 1938's annual fund-raising efforts. His regular letters to classmates stand as textbook studies in the subtle art of development communications, and his gentle pitches for contributions were always alive with reported details of contemporary Harvard, as his charge in 2010 declares: "Step back. Get out of the way. Support ... in every way possible." Bill's words—the generous words*

*of a grand old man, secure in his place and eager to help new genera-
tions excel—echo his life's creed and his life's work: "Keep the light
shining brightly." Indeed.*

*In retirement, Bill could be counted on to do favors for the legions
of St. Paul's alumni and parents he had come to know. For example, an
SPS parent who served as a trustee of the Windsor School in
Darnestown, Maryland, invited him to deliver this graduation speech.*

M R. WILDEMAN, members of the faculty, the Board
of Trustees, parents, friends, students, and most
particularly, members of the graduating class: Our principal focus today is on graduating seniors, as it should be.
But there are "graduating parents" present as well.
I would like to stop one moment, to ask parents to stand
and be recognized.

Graduating seniors: congratulations. What an exciting
time this is for you. What a satisfying time. Days and
weeks and months of work and hard effort are concluded.
Today you will receive a diploma, indicating successful
completion of years of study. Now it is all over.

Is it necessary at this point to have a speech? Let me
assure you, in the words used by Henry VIII to his first
wife, Catherine of Aragon: "I won't keep you long."

Yes, the program calls for an address at this time.
Shortly, you will have the opportunity of judging my comments and me. I hope the verdict will not be that of
a woman who had just heard her priest, on Sunday morning, preach on the subject of the joys of raising large families. She turned to her neighbor and said, "I wish I knew
as little about that subject as that young man."

179

One of the greatest statues of Michelangelo, that of a young man, was never finished. Michelangelo began work on a huge block of marble, pounding and chipping away, depicting the youth, David. But he never finished the statue. What remains, what we can see today, is a young man seeming to emerge from the marble, trying to free himself and to move into manhood, but forever held back, imprisoned for all time.

For me, that statue has always been a vivid symbol of the experience of youth in the high school years. The central theme is struggle. Partial success is evident, for clearly a young person of abilities and attributes is there. Yet much remains to be accomplished. The full person has yet to take the stage.

As we congratulate graduating seniors for many successful learnings and many satisfactory experiences, I would ask, what is the most important among all that you have learned? No one can know for sure, of course, but I want to make a suggestion.

Let me tell you about Isaac Stern, now seventy-four years old (and the finest violinist in the world). Stern was born in Russia. As an infant he was brought to Los Angeles, where at age three he began the study of the violin, continuing his studies, as the years went by, in New York and Europe. For years he has been considered one of the world's greatest musicians.

Recently Stern was asked, "Who among your several violin teachers was the best? Who had the most influence on you?" After a moment Stern named his teacher for three years, starting when he was eight years old. Why was he the best? Stern replied, "He helped me learn how to teach myself."

The point here is that individuals can be taught many things, some elementary, some complicated, but there comes a time when self-teaching must take over.

Abraham Lincoln did not learn from others how to lead this country in its greatest crisis, the Civil War. General Eisenhower made final decisions on the invasion of Normandy in 1944, having prepared for much at West Point and in his early life—but not for that momentous decision. Henri Matisse taught himself, late in life, to make cutouts of colored paper and to arrange them in pleasing order—there are magnificent examples of this work at the National Gallery which I hope you have studied.

Yes, the capacity to teach oneself is one of life's most powerful abilities. Graduating seniors, you can think of many things you have learned in the past three or four years. I suggest the most important part of your education is that you have learned, to one degree or another, how to teach yourself.

I want to suggest that you use this learning in the next several years in a particular way: to consider, from your experiences, what kind of a person you would like to be, and then to become that person. Each student who graduates from this school today, in moving to another community or school next year, has the unique opportunity of changing himself or herself; of altering habits and life patterns and the public face presented to others, so that in reputation, and in the thoughts of others, she or he can become quite a different person from what she or he has been before.

What happens to each of us, in the school where we spend our first years, is that we become a definite person. Others come to have specific expectations of us. Then we grow. We have experiences. We begin to see possible new life patterns for ourselves.

But, alas, we also discover it is extremely difficult for us to move affirmatively to a new self because our friends hold us firmly in their thoughts to what we have been. An interesting writer, Jerzy Kosinski, called this situation hell in his book *Being There*. He wrote, "Hell is the inability to escape from others who prove and prove again to you that you are as they see you."

The uniqueness of school graduation is that we leave those people behind. We move from one community to another, and thereby we gain the opportunity of starting all over, from the beginning.

One of my college roommates, long ago, acted on this principle for some months. He believed that meeting a person for the first time gave him an opportunity to try out a new personality. He carefully considered various kinds of roles for himself, from aggressive to meek, from studious to carefree. And he lived each of these roles for a few hours. Following each such experiment, he had a period of appraisal, to consider how effective he had been. How much he learned is not really the point here. Rather, I would suggest the willingness to experiment, to cast aside rigidities in one's personality, to test oneself under various pressures and conditions, and above all, not to assume that whatever it is I am, I am what I must remain—these are the important aspects of this man's experimentations.

Graduating seniors, you will be elsewhere next year. You are filled now with excitement and curiosity and anticipation about new activities and new experiences. I am suggesting that you study yourself: your attitudes, your point of view, your personality, your habits. Now is the time to consider change for yourself. Now is the time in your life when you can have a fresh start, if you want to.

Like Michelangelo's David, you have emerged from the marble, part way. I think it is significant that you can be your own Michelangelo. You can determine the final contours of your physical being and of your personality.

"My teacher helped me learn how to teach myself," said Isaac Stern.

Graduating seniors: congratulations. And the best of good luck to each of you.

—*Windsor School, May 29, 1993*

The Man Who Cured Polio

"Give credit where it's due" was surely a nostrum that Bill approved, especially if the one entitled to the credit was an alumnus of St. Paul's and of Harvard (by way of Yale College). Albeit twenty years Bill's senior, John Enders was such a one.

To the Editor: Jonas Salk, praised in your June 24 obituary for bringing polio under control, was "never, however, elected to the National Academy of Sciences of the United States." The Nobel Prize "eluded" him. The person responsible for one of the most significant discoveries of the 20th century, you imply, should have received a Nobel.

The scientist responsible was awarded a Nobel Prize: John Enders. And, though you appear to be mystified, the scientific community understands these developments. For years, experimentation seeking a polio vaccine was limited by the scarcity of the cultural medium in which experiments could be performed. Enders, a Harvard researcher, discovered a way, as you write, of "growing viruses in animal-cell tissue cultures in the laboratory."

Enders realized that, with a plentiful supply of experimental materials, he could expect to develop a vaccine for polio in two to ten years. Was there a way to hasten the process? Enders convened a meeting of representatives of the ten leading laboratories working on the problem, including Salk. He described his new process and suggested that every laboratory make use of it in a mass search for the answer. He also suggested that when any laboratory found a promising vaccine, a meeting of the ten laboratories be held to announce the discovery as the joint work of everyone.

Seven months later Salk, unilaterally, announced "his" discovery of the polio vaccine. It is not by chance, or a mistake, that the Nobel Prize "eluded" Salk, nor that he was not elected to the National Academy of Sciences.

Enders was held in highest respect for his magnanimous action, which, by hastening the discovery of the polio vaccine, saved thousands of people from death or crippling illness.

—New York Times, *published July 1, 1995*

On Smoking

In so many matters, Bill was an adherent of Ludwig Mies van der Rohe's modernist maxim: less is more. When I visited with him in April 2012—after spending some time at St. Paul's—I asked him about how the school, like so many other places in our common life, had become a virtual smoke-free zone. Some time later he sent me this charming recollection of his approach to the question of smoking and health, a reminder of the enduring reality that it's always the forbidden fruit that's most attractive.

FROM EARLIEST DAYS, as far as I know, the use of tobacco by students at St. Paul's School was prohibited. In my understanding, this rule was considered one of the major matters in the school's direction of student conduct. Breaking the smoking rule was viewed as a serious breach of conduct. Repeated breaking of the rule, in my experience, resulted in the dismissal of several students I knew well.

In 1964 the Surgeon General's report on smoking was issued, pointing out serious health consequences for use of tobacco in the general population. The report received wide publicity and had great influence: smoking rates in the United States dropped. But they did not drop as much as the scientific community thought wise and mandatory.

The fact that SPS had a major rule against the use of tobacco conflicted with the fact that voluntarily learning not to use tobacco should be a part of a general set of objectives for the teenage years. How do you teach the young voluntarily not to use tobacco when you command them not to?

I wrestled with this issue, talking with the vice rectors, finally the members of the Student Council. By happy coincidence, there were no smokers on the council. A conclusion became paramount: one of the most important gifts SPS could present to students, when they eventually reached the age of forty and beyond, was to be living without an addiction to tobacco. This objective assumed great importance in my thinking.

I changed the SPS rule to allow use of tobacco by students under two conditions. First, a letter to me from their parents giving their child permission to smoke in this new school environment. Second, smoking was permitted only in certain times and places, principally outdoors at the four corners of the school—prohibiting random use, in other words.

The faculty and council then went into full activity mode, securing films and posters, writers and speakers, planning chapel activities, and on and on. They waged a real battle to convince everyone not to smoke. During the process, several faculty members, hitherto heavy smokers, gave up tobacco.

In the first year there were 197 students out of 495 who had permission from their parents to smoke. In my last year, 1981–82, there were only three students with such permission. We won.

Shortly after announcing the new rules, I saw a friend who, I had always suspected, was a frequent smoker before the rule change. I said, "Joe, you probably are very happy." He looked at me in feigned surprise and asked, "What are you talking about, Mr. Oates?" I referred to his freedom to smoke at any time. His answer: "Mr. Oates, you don't understand. I have not had a cig since this rule was changed. I did not like smoking. I enjoyed breaking a small rule." I thought silently, one soul saved. I hope.

—Summer 2012

Harvard Letter

It may seem slightly incongruous to include this letter from Bill to his Harvard class in a volume devoted to St. Paul's. But for him, Harvard and St. Paul's were always tightly connected. Further, this letter is not only typical of Bill's communication with his "other" educational family, but so well conceived that it might serve as a model for any alumni fund-raising communiqué. It is brief, appealing, compelling— small wonder his class at Harvard has responded in record numbers for many years.

To Members of the Harvard College Class of 1938: They've arrived! First-year students, freshmen/ women, and they are everywhere. With ideas and objectives and questions and confidence—from all parts of the country. And the globe.

Harvard Square, Cambridge, 8.26.10. Small family units: Father dressed for the July beach, ready for three sets of tennis. Mother in carefully chosen dress, summer straw hat big enough to provide the wearer, and all nearby, with welcome shade from the sun still warm in late August. And offspring, the child (son or daughter) looking as though this couple most certainly belonged to someone else—eyes flashing, eager, curious, confident, ready to continue a fast run through life, with a new set of challenges and opportunities.

Sometimes, pairs of students only. One, of confident manner, who always, up to now anyway, has conquered every life challenge his or her mother or uncle could devise. The other, gazing into space, reflecting: this really isn't what I expected to find at Harvard.

Here is a happy, smiling individual, clearly pleased with himself, who appears to have just talked a professor (one with a widely recognized national reputation) into admission to a highly selective seniors-only seminar—a professor quick to recognize accomplishment and interest and ambition, a professor always ready to enlist another research assistant in his work.

Ready. Set. Go.

In October 2010 what's an alumnus to make of it all? That's easy. Praise God that life's cycles continue. Step back. Get out of the way. Cheer, and support the Class of 2014 in every way possible. Prepare to count the multiple achievements that are coming from this remarkable class and from other young students. Harvard: a significant heritage, a center of learning. The university: bequeathed to the world by scribes and scholars in Europe's Middle Ages. Hurrah. It's a great light. Keep the light shining brightly.

—Bill, 2010

Reflections on
William Armstrong Oates

At the time of Bill's retirement, in 1982, the Horae *carried an account of his achievements, written by Richard Lederer, a longtime English teacher (and tennis coach) who would become a nationally known commentator on English usage and the foibles of our tangled tongue. Lederer's humorous but heartfelt essay gives Bill's tenure its due, both as to theory and practice, with the light touch for which he was celebrated.*

BILL OATES, eighth Rector of St. Paul's School, has always been lavish in praising others and a bit shy and embarrassed when others praise him. Therefore, in expressing the appreciation of a grateful School for Bill's forty years of service and twelve years as Rector, I shall begin by talking about another educator and, perhaps, through indirection find direction out.

Once there was a fellow who decided that he wanted to become a headmaster by starting his own school. He published an impressively appointed catalogue that proclaimed how deeply he loved children and how much individual attention each student in his school would receive. Then he set about supervising the building of

191

the school. Every day he would go to the campus to watch the construction of the buildings and the landscaping of the grounds. Finally, all was completed except for the laying of a long cement path that ran through the center of the plant. The masons applied the cement, and the path lay glistening in the sunshine. Just as it was beginning to dry, a car pulled up to the curb, and out jumped an excited little boy, apparently a prospective student, who squealed with delight and scampered down the path, splattering cement all over the lawn.

The headmaster started to quiver, grabbed hold of the boy, and began beating him over the head. At this point, the boy's mother stormed out of the car, huffed up to the headmaster, and complained, "My dear sir, your catalogue boasts about how much you love children, yet here you are beating up my son! How do you explain that?" Replied the headmaster: "My dear madam, I may love children in the abstract, but not in the concrete."

Bill Oates loved children not only in the abstract, but also in the concrete, even if that love meant that they would often splatter cement or music or paint or dance on the lawns. Bill Oates knew that during his rectorship St. Paul's School would educate the first generation of students in history who would live the majority of their lives in the twenty-first century. He knew that such a prospect required the richest of curricula, at the center of which was man, the creator of religious myths and symbols; mathematical, scientific, and linguistic concepts; historical, social, and psychological systems; and visual and aural beauty and order from the swirl of life.

Bill also knew that an education from the neck up was but half an education. He realized that if you close down your heart, your mind cannot stay open for very long. From the center of his rectorship shone the light of Paul's statement in his First Letter to the Corinthians, which Bill quoted in Chapel on several occasions:

> If I speak in the tongues of men and of angels, but have not love, I am a noisy gong or a clanging cymbal. And if I have prophetic powers, and understand all mysteries and all knowledge, and if I have all faith, so as to remove mountains, but have not love, I am nothing.

In his January 8, 1978, Chapel talk, Bill clarified Paul's message by saying, "Paul is stating that love must be present in our every act, or our acts are without value. We remember that the word 'love' embraces intellectual, moral, and spiritual qualities such as good will, brotherliness, and friendship."

Bill Oates followed Paul's advice and sought to create, in his rectorship, a ministry of love. As carefully as he attended to every aspect of the School's operations, he was never too busy to see to the needs of each individual student. Whenever he announced the outstanding achievement of a student or the results of a student's transgressions, his eyes would brim with tears because he truly shared that student's joy or that student's pain. When the *Pelican*'s roving reporter asked the community, "What will you remember most about Mr. Oates?" one student said, "I will always remember how understanding he has been to me and to all of us students. His encouragement has profited so many students during the years."

At a dance held in the Oateses' honor this past spring, Bill was presented with a scroll, signed by the student body, that read: "To William A. Oates from the students of St. Paul's School, in appreciation for his leadership as Rector." When I asked Bill if he would pose for a *Pelican* picture with the scroll, he requested that the picture taking be delayed until Jean returned to School later that week so that they both could be photographed.

Here is one clue as to why Bill Oates loved students as easily as he breathed. He was and is so quintessentially a family man that all students at St. Paul's School were his sons and daughters. As a devoted husband and father, so loving of Margaret and Jean and his three sons—Bill, Jim, and Tom—his empathy for students was a natural and beautiful extension of his own life. No wonder that one of his favorite prayers was:

> Grant, O Lord, That in all the joys of life
> We may never forget to be kind.
> Help us to be unselfish in friendship,
> Thoughtful of those less happy than ourselves,
> And eager to bear the burdens of others;
> Through Jesus Christ our Saviour.

Bill Oates loved St. Paul's School in the abstract and in the concrete. For forty years his life was fired by a Platonic idea of perfect schoolness, and he rose every morning at 4:00 A.M. to labor on and make that vision live in this little corner of New England. That Bill and Jean virtually never missed a Saturday night open house at the Rectory in twelve years is an outward and visible sign of a seven-day-a-week labor of love. In "The Oatessy: An Epic Poem in Honor of Mr. Oates," the student poets sang:

> Each week our sovereign king and queen
> Throw ope their palace wide.
> There guests may dine on cookies
> Till they're feeling sick inside.

As one respondent to the *Pelican* poll commented, "I will remember his dreams and the energy he had to make them come true."

Even a brief listing of some of the items that Bill has written about in his Annual Reports, 1971–1981, indicates the scope of achievements during his rectorship: the Development Office, the Sixth Form year, the move of the Alumni Association to Concord, the arrival of girls, academic requirements, the disciplinary process, Form Agents, Human Relations, the demolition of the Lower School, School Year Abroad, Independent Study, the dress code, female trustees, the faculty internship program, the admissions process, the Faculty Leadership Committee, intervisitation, record giving by the Parents and Alumni Funds, Bob Duke and the Fund for SPS, the arts and the Performing Arts Buildings, creative ambiguity and personal growth, victories at the Henley Regatta, celebration of the School's 125th Anniversary, and the *Daedalus* symposia and publications.

Most recently, Bill has spearheaded a program at St. Paul's that encourages all students and faculty to become computer literate so that they may partake as joyfully as possible of the fruits of our civilization. Oates likes to keep up with the times. (He reads it every week.) An issue on computers had him caught by their mystique. He instantly decided that his students should partake. "One-sided educations / Don't well-rounded adults make" ("The Oatessy").

Even as Bill and Jean departed the grounds for their home in Kennebunk, Maine, the School workers were busily digging trenches for an updated telephone system and "pointing" the Schoolhouse, that is, drilling out the old mortar and replacing it with new material in order to buttress the building. Now there's as vivid an emblem, a metaphor, and a symbol as one could ask for. The goodly heritage of Bill Oates's rectorship is a school crosshatched by diverse and complex lines of communication, knitting together a vibrant community, and a School whose structures are solid and strong—in the abstract and in the concrete.

—*Richard Lederer,* Alumni Horae, *Summer 1982*

Envoi

This last piece appears here out of chronological order, not only because Bill deserves the last word but because these thoughts, from a chapel talk early in his rectorship, sum up his typical blend of gravity and whimsy. His enduring belief in the power of the simplest expressions of human connection—a handshake, a hello—exemplified his determination, in the words of the old school prayer, to make St. Paul's "in deed and in truth" a Christian school, to assure that none who come there may go away unimproved, that none may be afraid or ashamed to be God's faithful servants.

AT CHAPEL ONE DAY last year I told you a story about the school's telephone answering service. Some of you may remember the story, but I am going to repeat it this morning. Not because many of you need instruction about how to use our telephones. Rather, because this story illustrates something we all need to remember about friendship and thoughtfulness.

Several years ago, when the school installed a new telephone service providing internal dialing to various offices and places, everything went along splendidly during the day. But at night and on weekends, when the school number was handled by an answering service, there were difficulties. People complained that they could not make connections to receive incoming calls on the school line.

Upon investigation, the following situation turned up. When an outside call had been received, the answering service would dial one of the school numbers to tell the person he had a call. The service would say, "Please dial 88 to get the call." The individual would then dial 88 but fail to make the connection. The reason was simple. He did not also say hello.

What was happening was that a dial to number 88 did actually make the connection. Then there were two people on the line, one perhaps in New York, one here, each waiting for the other to say something. How they could not hear each other breathe, I never will know. But after a period of silence, one or the other would hang up, and the frustrating complaint would come back that the connection had not been made.

We made a small change in directions for the answering service. The operators were asked thereafter to say: "Dial 88 and say hello." People began to do so. Telephone connections were made, and the problem disappeared.

I tell you this because I think part of our human situation is that we are not saying hello to each other enough. That is, we are not reaching out to another person with a gesture. Too often, we are waiting. Too often we wait for the other person to make the beginning. I do not mean to suggest, of course, that substantial friendships will have been attained if only we begin speaking to each other. There is much more than that to friendship.

Friendship calls for acceptance of the other individual: full, total acceptance of him as he is. Full support and reassurance. Further, a friend stands ready to give help when asked. And occasionally he gives help and advice when these are not asked for. From friends I receive acceptance of myself. Reassurance that, in spite of the imperfections I know about myself, I am accepted without reservations. And I know I shall receive the help I need from my friends. Equally, I offer acceptance and reassurance and help to my friends.

No, substantial friendship is not just a matter of saying hello to others. But think for a moment: How can two people become friends unless they begin by speaking to each other? How can two people begin to know each other, unless they reach out to each other? The common strand that binds friendship and thoughtfulness is this quality of stretching out. It is for me to take the initiative. It is my move. I am the one to act.

This school is becoming a better place for each of as we extend our friendship to others. As we go to our homes on Thursday, we will find many opportunities to stretch out to others. To reach out with friendship to many: families, our parents and brothers and sisters who look forward so eagerly to our return.

We are different today. We are not the same people who came to school in January. We have grown and changed. I think, then, there is something that each of us can do, right now, in this place and at home. Each of us can make a greater effort to reach out to other people. We can begin by saying hello. We can acknowledge that in saying hello we are stretching out to others. We are offering friendship. And we can then follow, with ourselves. This we can do, today, as individuals. Dial 88 and say hello!

Let us pray.

Heavenly Father, for all thy goodness to us, we bless and praise thy holy Name;

For the beauty of this good earth, for the loveliness of flowers and changing seasons, for trees in winter darkly etched against a steel-gray sky, for racing clouds and starry nights;

For our friends and all the friendliness which has blessed our lives;

For human love which admits us so intimately into thy divine presence;

For life itself with all its glory, its challenge, its opportunity.

Keep us close to thee, we pray thee, that none of life be wasted; and make us channels and agents of thy good will in a troubled world.

Amen.

—Last Morning Chapel of the Winter Term, 1972

About the Authors

William A. Oates

*is the rector emeritus of St. Paul's School. His twelve-year
tenure was perhaps the most transformative of any
headmaster's, as he oversaw the start of coeducation and
brought the arts into the curriculum. Twice widowed, and a
nonagenarian, he lives outside Boston near his sons.*

Todd S. Purdum

is the national editor of Vanity Fair. *A graduate
of St. Paul's School, he went on to Princeton and then
to* The New York Times *where he worked as
a copyboy, Washington correspondent, and Los Angeles
bureau chief. He lives in Washington, D.C., with his wife,
Dee Dee Myers, the political consultant and former
White House press secretary, and their two children.*

CREDITS

PHOTOGRAPHS

Bradford F. Herzog: *frontispiece; 100 (both), 102 bottom, 104–7*

C. H. King III: *101*

David Powers: *97*

St. Paul's School Archives: *98–99, 102 top, 103, 108*

PRODUCTION

Copy edited by Duke Johns

Designed and typeset by Robert L. Wiser

Printed on 80-pound Mohawk Superfine
in Hollis, New Hampshire, by Puritan Capital

Colophon

Views from the Rector's Porch
is composed in Requiem Text, created by Jonathan Hoefler
in 1994, a font family that embodies the spirit of
Renaissance Humanism. Hoefler closely modeled his
typefaces on lettering of the celebrated Italian calligrapher
Ludovico Vincentino degli Arrighi (1480–1527), whose
work reflected a revival of interest in the geometric
proportions of classical inscriptions. The decorative
cartouches in the section titles were inspired by designs
of Arrighi's contemporaries, Giovanni Battista Palatino
and Vespansiano Amphiareo.